Clement Mansfield Ingleby

The Still Lion

An Essay towards the Restoration of Shakespeare's Text

Clement Mansfield Ingleby

The Still Lion
An Essay towards the Restoration of Shakespeare's Text

ISBN/EAN: 9783337063566

Printed in Europe, USA, Canada, Australia, Japan

Cover: Foto ©Thomas Meinert / pixelio.de

More available books at **www.hansebooks.com**

THE STILL LION.

AN ESSAY

TOWARDS

The Restoration of Shakespeare's Text.

BY

C. M. INGLEBY, M.A., LL.D.,

OF TRINITY COLLEGE, CAMBRIDGE, FOREIGN SECRETARY TO THE ROYAL SOCIETY OF
LITERATURE, LONDON.

REPRINTED, WITH ADDITIONS, FROM THE SECOND ANNUAL
VOLUME OF THE GERMAN SHAKESPEARE SOCIETY.

ὥρχθηθ᾽, οἵαις αἰκίαισιν
διακναιόμενος τὸν μυριετῆ
χρόνον ἀθλιέσω᾽

PROMETHEUS VINCTUS, 93–95.

LONDON:

TRÜBNER & CO., 57 & 59, LUDGATE HILL.

1874.

A COPY OF

THIS ESSAY

IS PRESENTED TO EACH MEMBER OF

The New Shakspere Society.

———————•———————

ERRATA.

ADVERTISEMENT.

The following essay originally appeared in the Second Annual Volume of the German Shakespeare Society, where it received as much notice as it deserved. The late Alexander Dyce devoted to it three pages of his *Glossary*, forming volume ix of his last edition of Shakespeare. Of late years the author has received so many inquiries about it, and applications for it, that he has revised and enlarged it for an English edition; and it is now for the first time printed as a separate work.

The present edition substantially reproduces the original essay, 'enlarged to almost as much again as it was' mainly by the addition of seven critical discussions in Chapter iv and of nine in Chapter v.

The *short copies* which in 1867 were issued for presentation had a special title-page bearing a motto from the *Prometheus Vinctus*. This motto is retained, and an excursus, in justification of it, is prefixed to the main work.

The title of the essay, though eccentric, is significant as well as mysterious, and is sufficiently explained in the opening paragraph. All the leonine allusions (for the noble beast, like King Charles's head in David Copperfield, was always emerging) have been sentenced to capital punishment; and the execution will serve the beneficent purpose of a notice-board bearing the warning, *Cave Leonem.* We have heard that the votaries of the Olympian Sire* (who, it must be known, has in these days taken Mrs Grundy to wife) have been greatly scandalised by the allegorical title and by-play of this work. The mode in which the leonine allusions are here presented will serve to warn off over-sensitive readers from the offending regions of allegory, which we sorrowfully own—but in the geological sense—to constitute the "great fault" of the ensuing essay.

* See p. x. l. 12.

CONTENTS.

a 2

JUSTIFICATION OF THE GREEK MOTTO.

EVEN the few who care for both the *integrity* and the *preservation* of Shakespeare's works will form but a very faint notion of the subject of this preliminary essay from the motto. What can be the outrage which threatens either the one or the other? Are not his works, like 'the lexicons of ancient tongues,' 'comprised in a few volumes,' of which millions of copies exist? Yes, indeed; but are they 'immutably fixed?' Nay, more, is it at all likely that they will be immutably fixed? That is the doubt which suggested the following remarks. The works of Shakespeare were manifestly written to serve his own personal ends, or, at most, to serve the narrow ends of his own generation; and yet, in a higher sense, they were written for all time—to subserve the pleasure and profit of ages to come. Ben Jonson summed this up in the famous line—much staled, and generally misquoted—

> He was not *of* an age, but *for* all time.

Now Jonson meant to say of Shakespeare that he *was* both *for* an age and *for* all time, which the line, as it is often misquoted, is made to contradict,[*] but also that he was not *of* an age: meaning thereby that, unlike his compeers, he was unconventional and catholic. We have a proverbial saying, ' He is a nice man *for* a small tea-party '—exquisite expansion of the *petit maitre*! A man may be that, without being *of* the tea-party; he may likewise be *of* the tea-party without being that. The early Christians were exhorted to be *in* the world, not *of* the world. St Paul, for example, was not *of* the world; yet he was *for* the world; and many a man *of* the world lives *for* himself, and not *for* the world. Things more distinct than *of* and *for* it were hard to find. Shakespeare was in the world of his own day; but he was not of it he lived in an intellectual sphere above it, and so lived and wrote for it, and for all time.

Even we of the 19th century, or 4th A.S., *know* very little what will be. We have great faith in the destiny of Shakespeare's works, and *believe* that, if they are preserved entire, they will be a most important element among those forces which go to mould the English of the future; and that what Æschylus

---

* The most inexcusable case is that of Mr John Leighton's 'Official Seal for the National Shakespeare Committee of 1864,' the scroll at the base of which bears the misquotation—

Not for an age, but for all time

is to us Shakespeare will be to those who speak a tongue as yet unknown, when the English of Shakespeare is bound in death.

A living language is like the mythic Proteus. It is a fluxion : no photography is swift and sharp enough to catch and arrest any one of its infinite and infinitesimal phases. But as, in the old fable, Proteus caught basking on the seashore became oracular, so when at last a language dies, it not only becomes a dry logical instrument, but an oracle, which reveals the history of a people long after every material trace of their existence has vanished from the earth.—— (*Englishman's Magazine*, Jan. 1865.)

The language we speak and write is not perfectly identical with that employed by Shakespeare. English speech has moved on, and is still moving on towards the goal ; and in a period which is incalculable, not for its length, but for want of exact *data*, it will be as dead as Zend, Sanscrit, Greek, or Latin. It is of no use lamenting this destiny, for it is inevitable. By no other course can a language attain to the rank of a classic tongue. Happily, when a language is dead, its literature may survive. How many literatures have been swallowed up already is only known to Him who created us. To deal with two only of those languages, we have reason to be thankful that the sentence executed on Hebrew and Greek spared so large and so grand a fraction of their literatures : Job, David, Isaiah, Ezekiel, Jeremiah, Homer, Æschylus, Sophocles, Euripides, Aristophanes !

Æschylus had a narrow escape. He was judged an immortal before his death. The late Mr Charles Knight thought Shakespeare was judged so too ; but we doubt if all the evidences that can be gathered from the literatures of the 16th and 17th centuries would prove that he was thought essentially superior to Marlow, Chapman, Jonson, Beaumont, or Fletcher—all men *of the age*. Even the most illiterate Greeks who were privileged to live and move in the Athens of Pericles knew that they had a demi-god among them. Every soul in that mighty auditory knew his Æschylus 'was not of an age, but for all time.' Nay, more ; Æschylus was twice as industrious a writer as Shakespeare. He created, and published in that vast arena, where from twenty to thirty thousand persons were always found to enjoy a foretaste of immortality, *twice* as many tragedies as Shakespeare wrote plays. Above 70 dramas were the pledges of their writer's earthly immortality ; yet only seven survive. When the first Alexandrine Library was burnt, it is said that nearly 70 single exemplars of his tragedies perished. Happily for us, the immortality of Æschylus was guaranteed by the fact that imperfect copies of seven dramas existed in other libraries. Had they been perfect, our Greek scholarship would have been more imperfect ; for nothing short of imperfection in *such* works could have called into healthy activity the powers of our best Grecians. But only think what a narrow escape this great writer had ! But for the extant seven, we could have known nothing of him but at second-hand. At most we might have known that the great Sophocles had a contemporary greater than himself ; but we could have had no sufficient evidence to estimate the majesty and sublimity of him whose works had fallen a victim to the ambition of Cæsar.

Now, against such a catastrophe as that Shakespeare is amply secured. Thank God, there are no single exemplars of any work of his. Compared with the great Greek his works are not so vast—37 plays, 2 long poems, a noble collection of sonnets, and a small volume of 'Remains,' constitute our whole stock-in-trade.

But of the existing exemplars of each work the name is Legion! At any price from 1s. up to £100 the book-fancier may appropriate a complete copy of Shakespeare's works. The fount is open to all: come, all ye thirsty souls—be ye prince, poet, gentleman, artisan, labourer, tramp, or what not, here's the work for your money. Here are Warne's Chandos edition, 8vo, in boards, for 1s.; Dicks's edition, 8vo, stitched, for 1s., and in boards, for 2s.; Lenny's edition, 12mo, for 2s. 6d., or if you can afford another 6d. here is Keightley's smaller edition, 12mo, and the Blackfriar's edition, 8vo. You had better pay 3s. 6d., and then you may have a better choice—the Globe edition, 8vo, Mrs Cowden Clarke's edition, 8vo, or Lenny's selected edition, 12mo. Besides these there is Gray Bell's edition, 8vo, 3s. 10d., which is now reduced; and when you get up to 4s. or 5s. you may have the pick of a score of one-volume editions, and so forth, till we mount up to those costly monuments of human enterprise, Boydell's illustrated edition and Mr Halliwell's folio edition, and, lastly, the original first folio edition, accessible only to princes and merchant-princes. A thousand Alexandrine conflagrations would not at this present time burn up Shakespeare.

No: it is from no such danger that we have to rescue Shakespeare; it is from a destruction now in progress, and the cause is latent, insidious, slow, and sure. The mere destruction of copies is more than compensated by new impressions; but it is precisely because there is this succession, this constant and unstaying process of supplantation and substitution, that the immortality of Shakespeare is in jeopardy. If this cause shall continue, it is demonstrable that Shakespeare's immortality can be guaranteed by only one event—the continued practice of reprinting verbatim the First Folio Edition. It makes one tremble to think that but for photography there was a bare possibility (perhaps a very small one) of Shakespeare faring like Æschylus. It is almost certain that after the lapse of ages every copy which was in existence in the 16th, 17th, 18th, and 19th centuries, and all which are now extant, will be utterly destroyed. We say Shakespeare's immortality is only guaranteed by the multiplication of copies. Now, from what exemplars are they made? There is a cause of corruption constantly in operation which must sooner or later revolutionize the whole text, viz., the practice of modernizing the old language, so as to bring it down to the standard of the English of 300 years later. Where is this to stop? Clearly, nowhere. Language finds no arrest; it must grow or die. The innocent-looking little modifications which we now introduce into Shakespeare on the plea of textual misprinting will sooner or later themselves require modernizing. No part of the text is safe against these well-intentioned perversions; and in the mean while what becomes of Shakespeare? The one fact which bids fair to secure him against this fate is the multiplication of copies by photography from the folio of 1623. There is no one deed in the history of Shakespeare-literature which deserves more thanks than the recent reprint of the first folio by the photolithographic process. Few know (as the writer of this work does) the stupendous difficulties under which the first promoter of this special work laboured. It were easy to name several gentlemen who were employed in the various departments of this production, to all of whom great credit is due for the conscientious discharge of their several tasks; but when the history of that reprint is written, as written it will be, who will stand out as the originator and the finisher of the work? One there was who, at first with little aid and no sympathy, originated that reprint, and with infinite labour, miscarriage, vexation, and loss succeeded in carrying it to a successful issue; and his name is HOWARD STAUNTON.

To that gentleman is it due that Shakespeare is delivered from one source of destruction. One shoal is weathered: another is imminent; but it is one that can only acquire importance in the event of Mr Staunton suffering a final check-mate in this new chess-game, *i.e.*, in the event of all *verbatim* reprints of the first folio being destroyed.* This source of destruction is contingent only: but whatever it is let us diagnose it. It is here that Shakespeare appears in the character of the modern Prometheus. He has committed the heinous offence of endowing men with the πρὸς σέλας of heaven, the blaze of the fire of genius. For this the Olympian Sire, who seems to represent Persistent Conventionality, is angry, and he sends down on the Bard two ministers of vengeance. The destinies of Literature are committed to certain publishing coteries: these rule the Reviews; and the Reviews forge the thunderbolts of criticism, which at one time wound a Byron or a Shelley, and at another kill a Keats; or pour the vials of vengeance on an offending party; as once on the so-called Lake Poets. The mischief is, that *Freedom* and *Power*, the attributes of Zeus, belong (for a time) to those who have not the genius to appreciate the philosophy of mind and language, and thus *to integrate the fluxion of written speech*. Accordingly these Procrustean censors have determined, and seem determined to determine to all eternity, that the text of Shakespeare shall be measured by a standard which is hardly adequate to the criticism of Tennyson or Robert Browning. The English of Shakespeare in 10,000 places is not what now passes for good English; therefore say the censors, it must be made good English. In a small percentage of cases they allow the possibility of an obsolete phraseology; but not at all as to the mass. Where they do not and cannot understand him, he is assumed to have fallen a prey to his own impetuosity or carelessness, or to the blundering of a compositor, and it is their task to set him right. The sluice is thus opened, and Shakespeare's language is inundated with words and phrases, some of which, indeed, he might have used; but, so far as we know, did not use: the poetry and special sense are concurrently eliminated in every spot where the critic sets his mark; and instead of 'the text of Shakespeare,' England prints and publishes 'the text of Shakespeare *restored*.' *Restored!* The very word suggests a similar process applied to architecture: indeed, the modern mode of restoring Shakespeare cannot be better illustrated than by comparing him to such an edifice as Beverley Minster. Not only is something put in the place of what has fallen a victim to time and chance; but much of what remains of the old work is ruthlessly removed to make room for an imitation of the old work by some village stonemason, who has no knowledge of or feeling for his business.

But the parallel between Shakespeare and Prometheus may be worked out in greater detail. One motive to the persecution of greatness is the jealousy of excellence, a sentiment which is begot between the Sense of Inferiority and the Love of Power. To be confronted with an author whose works have stimulated in his admirers, for eight or nine generations, a passion of gratitude and worship,

---

* Our friend suffered another kind of 'final check-mate' during the printing of this work. He died on June 22nd, 1874.

and to find his works strange and uncouth, his phrases unusual, if not unintelligible, and his allusions obscure, is to suffer humiliation. The critic of conscious intellect and learning is offended that Shakespeare should have won a world of worshippers by works which he finds but imperfectly intelligible. He naturally seeks to disabuse those worshippers, to convict them of Fetish-worship, and to bring down their idol to their own level. He will at least show them *who* is a power in the world; he will explain and correct this writer, and banish to the limbo of oblivion whatever he cannot understand. As to the unfathomable, which some believe to be Shakespeare, he says, ' Away with it to the unfathomable abyss—like to like!' All the while the critic is getting, by a side wind, a considerable reputation for his disinterested, courageous, and sensible conduct. This battered idol is all very well for Buddha; but he is very ugly, and by your leave, the artist will mend his nose and transport him to the back garden. Or the Olympian plan shall be tried, which is preferable on the whole, seeing that (as Oceanus says to Prometheus) it is not profitable to kick against the pricks,* for in the world of letters the press is exposed to the goad of public opinion, and that Shakespeare is a demigod, and was an inspired poet, is a part of its creed. It is to be acknowledged, then, that this Promethean Shakespeare is a god; he had, it is allowed, great genius and power; he did give you fire from heaven, and teach you all arts. But look you, he is ungrammatical and profane, and had no knowledge of the classics, and his geography was very shaky. However, we think that much of this may have been caused by the blunders of reporters, copyists, and printers. So the god is taken captive by Zeus, the public press, and handed over to the tender mercies of two emissaries, not as of old, Strength and Force, but Dulness and Ignorance, and these have it in charge to manacle him hand and foot to the rock of Pedantry. But these gentlemen, though very *able* in their way, are not blacksmiths, so Hephæstus (Vulcan), the Philologer, is called in to help. A very unwilling and altogether unsympathizing agent is he. He tells them plainly, ' I really have not the heart to bind my fellow-god to this weather-beaten cliff. Yet I must on every account take heart for this business, for it is no trifle to disobey the orders of the Sire.' The prejudices of the Press infect him, and we find him clenching manacle after manacle on the suffering god; like Horne Tooke teaching us that Frenchmen are (according to Shakespeare) *brayed* in a mortar, or at least that Bertram was (Diversions of Purley, 1805, ii. 50); or like Mr F. J. Furnivall asserting that Timon's ' wappen'd widow' was merely wrapt or shrouded in her widow's weeds (*Athenæum*, May, 1873),† and many other things quite as absurd.

Philology, perverted and degraded, does the work of Conventionality, Dulness, and Ignorance, till at last Dulness gives Prometheus a left-handed compliment to his greatness—' How can mortals ever lighten thine agonies? By no true title do

---

* This expression, which occurs in the account of the Conversion of St Paul (Acts ix. 5), is nearly akin to those in the Prometheus and the Agamemnon. It sounds strangely out of place in sequence with our Lord's declaration; for it is evident that both the Lord and the Apostle could not at once be driver and driven. If St Paul were the persecutor the 'pursuer' it would not be in his power to 'kick against the pricks.' It is a relief to know that the phrase has little title to its place in the Latin Vulgate and our Authorized Version.

† We are glad to learn that our friend has withdrawn that explanation. Dr Stratmann, however, gives the same explanation of Shakespeare's ' wappen'd widow.'

the divinities call thee Prometheus; *for thou thyself wilt need a Prometheus to help thee to escape this work of craft.'* How true that is! None but the man of genius can really help Shakespeare. It is only the hero who discerns, and has power to enfranchise, the hero.

The truth is, that the Sire, as the Choragus says, is administering new conventions, μοχμοῖς νομοῖς· and wiping out those things which men used to think great, τὰ πρὶν πελώρια. Here is, indeed, the gist of the crime against Shakespeare. The continual ebb and flow of language, in its growth from the conventional to the classic, is the cause of all the evil that has befallen him. It is to the strong-armed and gentle-hearted Hephæstus that we must look for help. At present he is but lame—we know who has lamed him—but sooner or later those rivets will be undone; that transfixing bolt will be withdrawn; the idiom, idiotisms, and, above all, the idiasms of Shakespeare will be thoroughly understood, and so much that now goes by the board in all modern editions will be restored with intelligent reverence. This is the great work that is committed to all who have discernment or faith in the great and suffering hard.

In this case, the cause of Prometheus is the cause of our Mother Tongue. It is impossible to doubt that a great future is in store for the English language. A time must come when that language will be the language of half the world. Future literatures are bound up in its fate. Now, without exception, Shakespeare, of all who have expressed their thoughts in it, knew best how to use it. It is not from a county, a parish, or a household that a language becomes enriched and defined. It is rather from the works of great popular writers. Hence it is that language acquires healthy growth and development. We can readily see, then, how large a factor in the future of English will be the works of Shakespeare, and it is now a question for us whether that factor shall be of the sixteenth and seventeenth centuries, having Shakespeare's proper impress and power, or whether it shall be a stunted and modernised Shakespeare that is to have that influence. It is now a question for us, whether we shall take side with 'the Sire' (the public critic or popular press) or with Vulcan, freed from the tyranny of Zeus—whether the Promethean Bard, who has endowed us with so many heavenly gifts, shall be bound and impaled on the rock of pedantry or conventionalism, or whether he shall be free and powerful, as he is god-like and benevolent.

I say that question is for *us.* But who are we? It is little we can do against the tyranny of 'the Sire.' We may at least do our little without fearing his censure, or coveting his praise. Others may cast in their lot with him; may exalt Marlow, or even Addison, and depress Shakespeare; may sneer at the Promethean fire as George III. did, calling it 'poor stuff,' or scoff at Prometheus himself, as a late noble lord did, calling him 'Silly Billy.' We, for our parts, will take our stand with him against the criticasters and the detractors, and will not relax in our exertions to enfranchise Shakespeare; though it will not be our fortune to proclaim 'Prometheus Unbound;' 'for he that shall deliver is not yet.'

THE STILL LION.

E may say of Shakespeare's text what Thomas De Quincey said of Milton's:

'ON ANY ATTEMPT TO TAKE LIBERTIES WITH A PASSAGE OF *HIS*, YOU FEEL AS WHEN COMING, IN A FOREST, UPON WHAT SEEMS A DEAD LION; PERHAPS HE MAY *NOT* BE DEAD, BUT ONLY SLEEPING, NAY PERHAPS HE MAY NOT BE SLEEPING, BUT ONLY SHAMMING. * * * * You may be put down with shame by some man reading the line otherwise,'

or, we add, reading it in the light of more extended or more accurate knowledge.

Here lies the covert danger of emendation. It is true that the text of Shakespeare, as it comes down to us—"the latest seed of time"—in the folio 1623, as well as in the early quartos, is very corrupt. It is corrupt on two accounts. As to the text of the quartos, there was no proper editorial supervision, since the editions were intended merely for the accommodation of play-goers; the text was therefore imperfect in substance as well as in form. As to the text of the folio, the supervision of Messrs Heminge and Condell seems to have been confined to the selection of copies for the printers, Messrs Jaggard and Blount; and some of those were play-house copies, which had been curtailed for representation, and certain other were copies of quarto editions; while the correction of the press was probably left to the 'reader' of the printing-house,[*] who certainly could not have exercised any extraordinary vigilance in his vocation. Accordingly we have imperfect copies at first, and a misprinted text at last.

The corrupt and mutilated condition in which the Greek and Roman Classics, especially the Greek, have been handed down to modern times is the sufficient reason for that latitude of conjectural criticism which has been brought to bear on the ancient texts. If we had to deal with an English text which bore like evidences of dilapidation, we should naturally have recourse to the same means for its correction. But such is not the case with the works of any English author who has assumed the proportions of a classic: not Chaucer, nor Shakespeare, nor Milton, is a venerable ruin demanding restoration; though Shakespeare, far more than Milton, has suffered corruption, by the very nature of the vehicle to which he committed his thoughts; exactly as the 'Last Supper' of Leonardo da Vinci has incurred an amount of destruction which it

---

[*] Not improbably Edward Blount, Isaac Jaggard's partner See *Notes and Queries*, 2nd S. iii. 7.

might have escaped had it been painted on wood or on canvass. Such corruption, however, as infects the works of Shakespeare touches but comparatively small, and often isolated, portions of the text, offering no very serious obstacle to the general reader, who is not exacting or scrupulous in the interpretation of his author's phraseology. Patches of indictable nonsense, which have hitherto defied all attempts at elucidation, there are, as we shall soon see, in some of the plays ; but it is no very violent proceeding to regard them as parts of the inferior matter interpolated by the players or derived by Shakespeare from the older plays on which he founded his own. But the critical student is naturally intolerant of every unexplored obscurity and unresolved difficulty; and the editor who works for students as well as for general readers feels himself bound to apply to the text all available resources of criticism. The example of the ancient Classics, and the capital success which rewarded the vigilance and invention of the critics in that field, could not fail to determine the method on which the recension of Shakespeare was to be attempted by the verbal critics.

As the natural result, the text has been subjected to a conjectural criticism which owns no restraint and systematically violates every principle of probability and of propriety. Obsolete phraseology and archaic allusion are treated as cases of corruption: the language, instead of being restored or amended, is modernized and *improved :* and the idiom, instead of being expounded and illustrated, is accommodated to the prevailing grammatical stand-

ard. By this means more fatuous and incapable nonsense has been manufactured for Shakespeare than can
be found in any of the ancient copies of his plays.

The text of Milton, on the other hand, offers little or
no holding for the conjectural critic.* One might have
predicted that of all English texts it was the least likely to
have afforded congenial sport to a classical scholar intent
on havoc. But it was not so much the promise of the
covers, but the solicitations of exalted rank, that induced
the combative and tenacious old Master of Trinity, when
he had already earned his laurels as an editor of the
Classics, and ' won his spurs ' as a verbal critic of match-
less resource and felicity, even in the 69th year of his age,
to undertake the recension of *Paradise Lost*. As some

---

* The *systematic* departure from the ordinary spelling of the time
in the text of the *Paradise Lost* of 1667 has been noticed by De
Quincey. Mr B. M. Pickering says :

' At the end of the first edition of *Paradise Lost* we meet with what,
to a casual observer, would appear to be a very singular correction, *viz.*
Lib. 2. v. 414, " For *we* read *wee*." Even a tolerably attentive student
of the early editions of Milton might be at a loss what to make of this. It
is certain that *we* is to be met with in this edition of *Paradise Lost* quite
as often, or rather much oftener, with a single than with a double *e*. It
occurs as *we* in the very next line to that referred to in this errata.
The explanation is this :—that although in ordinary cases Milton is
accustomed to spell the pronouns *we*, *me*, *he*, *ye*, with a single *e*, when-
ever special emphasis is intended to be put upon them he makes a point
of writing *wee*, *mee*, *hee*, *yee*. Many other words are differently spelt
to what was then. or is now, usual, and this not in an uncertain manner, as is common in old books, but after a regular, unvarying system,
deliberately formed by Milton himself, and adopted upon choice and
afore-thought.' (From the Prospectus of A Reprint of the First Edition
of *Paradise Lost*.)

sort of self-justification he framed the hypothesis that Milton's text had suffered through the carelessness and also the invention of the scribe to whom it had been dictated by the blind bard. Bentley was a great man, and this work of his is great in its way. He mars his author with regal splendour, and we admire his learning and talents, while we deplore their misapplication, and deride his performance.

This reference to Milton, WHO IS ALSO A STILL LION, THRILLING INDEED WITH LIFE, BUT OFTEN DISSEMBLING HIS VITALITY, leads me to exhibit the salient contrasts between the two English classics of the seventeenth century. I will first consider the works themselves as intellectual achievements; secondly, the material vehicle of their transmission.

(1) Dramatic Literature, out of the very reason for its existence, is more within the compass of the ordinary understanding than an epic poem. Its appeal is to the common mind. If the people fail to catch the meaning of a dialogue or a soliloquy, it is a mere impertinence, how splendid soever may be its diction, or profound the reach of its thought. Shakespeare is, indeed, very strongly differenced from his contemporaries by the fervour of his imagination and his knowledge of human nature, as well as by the strength and range of his vocabulary; and certain portions of his works are pitched in as sublime a key as the epics of Milton. But on the whole the language of Shakespeare is more or less amenable to undisciplined good sense.

Milton, on the contrary, 'flies an eagle's flight,' and is quite out of the blank of the general aim. He is 'caviary to the general,' and the strongest common sense, without imagination and intellect, is quite at fault in the criticism of his greater works.

With this distinction in mind, the reason of Bentley's deplorable failure in attempting an edition of *Paradise Lost* is not far to seek. The work he had successfully done was in the field of the Greek and Latin Classics, the emendation of which, as that of our early dramatic literature, is generally within the range of that strong natural sense for which Bentley was so conspicuous: and this, complemented with his vast book-learning, was amply sufficient for his purpose. One almost wonders that he did not make the experiment on Shakespeare rather than on Milton; and it seems natural to fancy that, had he known in what relationship of marriage he stood to the Bard of Avon,* he would have been drawn to the recension of his great relative's works, and would have brought to the task that reverential affection which is so conspicuously absent from his notes on Milton.

(2) The difference in the 'material vehicle' consists in the difference between Dramatic Art and Literature. We must consider this at somewhat greater length. Disallowing Bentley's pretext, as a mere device for the indulgence of licentious criticism, which especially in the

---

* The relationship is easily stated though it is very remote. Shakespeare's granddaughter married (secondly) the brother of Mrs Bentley's grandfather.

case of Milton *sufflaminandus est*, it is plain that Milton's epics enjoyed the benefit of being printed, if not under the eye, at least under the direct superintendence, of their author; and we know, moreover, that he was fastidiously vigilant and accurate. We may be quite sure that the text contains but very few misprints, and that conjecture has no *locus standi* there. But how different was the case with the dramas of Shakespeare! Speaking of the textual vehicle only, we may be equally sure that the conjectural critic would have had 'the very cipher of a function' if those works had received the final corrections and editorial supervision of their author. They would still have been thronged with difficulties, and pestered with obscurities, taxing the utmost erudition and study of the editor, the greater number of which would have belonged to the class *historical*, consisting wholly of allusions to forgotten persons and events, and to obsolete habits and customs. Not a few, however, of those difficulties would have belonged to the class *grammatical*, demanding on the part of the expositor almost as much learning and research as the *historical* allusions in the text: for since the date of Shakespeare's *floruit* the English language has suffered no inconsiderable change, though much less than the habits and customs of the English people.

But Shakespeare died without, so far as we know, having made the attempt to collect and print his works. Of this fact an unnecessary difficulty has been made. A much more self-conscious genius than Shakespeare has himself given us the clue to its solution, a clue of which all writers, save Thomas Carlyle,[*] have failed to perceive the significance. Goethe confessed to Eckermann that he never reperused any of his poems when once it was completed and printed, unless impelled to the task by the demand for a new edition; and that he then read it with no self-complacency, but rather dissatisfaction. Why was this? Simply because he felt a *Widerwille*, or distaste, towards the offspring of his less matured self, by reason of its inadequacy to express his great ideal—the ' unbodied figure of the thought that gave 't surmised shape.' He had outgrown his own powers, in the grander sense of that phrase: never, like poor Swift, living to look back with wonder and horror on the glory of a genius that he owned no more, but prejudicially contrasting his past self with the greater present.

'As for what I have done,' he would repeatedly say to me, ' I take no pride in it whatever. Excellent poets have lived at the same time with myself, poets more excellent have lived before me, and others will come after me.' (Gespräche mit Goethe, 1836. Vol. i., p. 86. Feb. 19th, 1829. Oxenford's Translation.)

He had, seemingly, that very contempt for self-complacency which he attributes to Faust—

> ' Verflucht voraus die hohe Meinung,
> Womit der Geist sich selbst umfängt.'

Now Shakespeare wrote and issued under his own eye two poems as literature, and nothing else. The rest of his works, save his sonnets and minor pieces, were

---

[*] Consult his *Shooting Niagara, and after?*

written for representation on the boards, and as a simple matter of money-profit. Not faultless even as dramas, they must have fully answered his aim, which was purely mercenary, but not that grand ideal which dwelt 'deep down in his heart of hearts.' Hence he must have viewed them with some disaffection, (1) as not being in the best sense Literature ; (2) as being 'mere implorators of—mercenary, if not—unholy suits,' designed to catch the penny with the least pains ; (3) as being often hasty and inchoate, and always imperfect, attempts to realize his own ideal. From the effort of recasting and revising them he naturally shrunk. If he gave a thought to the probability of his works becoming his country's crowning glory, it might very reasonably have occurred to him, that no revision would be likely to guarantee them an exemption from the common lot which was not the due of their original merits. Of one thing we may be quite sure, that Shakespeare's good sense and honesty of purpose rendered him perfectly indifferent to that vanity of vanities which Goethe, in the speech from which a citation has already been made, calls 'das Blenden der Erscheinung,' for which so many a man of letters has sacrificed the calm and comfort of his life.

Be all that as it may, the fact is this, that the first collection of his plays was published six or seven years after his death ; and it is a matter of certainty that the folio of 1623 was printed from inaccurate quarto editions and mutilated stage-copies. This is the 'case' of those who advocate the rights of unlimited criticism; and we cordially make the concession, that our text needs emendation. But, before they can be permitted to conjecture, we require of them to find out where the corruptions lie. If a man's body be diseased, the seat of the disease can generally be determined between the patient and the doctor: in some cases, however, the malady baffles research and experiment.

In the case of Shakespeare's text, the diagnosis is infinitely perplexed: (1) from the multitude of obscurities and difficulties that beset it: (2) from the close resemblance that often subsists between those obscurities which spring from the obsolete language or the archaic allusions, and those which are wholly due to the misreading or misprinting of the text. Our healthy parts are so like our diseased parts, that the doctor sets about the medicinal treatment of that which needs no cure; and the patient's body is so full of those seeming anomalies, that his life is endangered by the multiplicity of agencies brought to bear on his time-worn frame.

What, if there are cases in which those κύριοι συνωμόται, archaic phraseology and textual corruption, unite their powers against us? Why, in such cases, it is most likely that the critic would be utterly baffled: that he would be unable to restore the lost integrity even by the combined forces of exposition and conjecture. Now it so happens that after all that contemporary literature and conjectural criticism could do for Shakespeare's immortal works, there is a residue of about thirty-five to forty passages which have defied all attempts to cure their immortal nonsense. Does it not seem likely that the perplexity in such cases is due to the joint action of those two sources of obscurity, and our inability to *persever* or discriminate the one from the other? We shall see. The *rintage* afforded by these remarks may be thus expressed. Conjectural criticism is legitimate; for it is needful to the perfection of the text: but no critic can be licensed to exercise it whose knowledge and culture do not guarantee these two great pre-requisites: (1) a competent knowledge of the orthography, phraseology, prosody, as well as the language of arts and customs, prevalent in the time of Shakespeare: (2) a refined and reverent judgment for appreciating his genius and learning.

The present time seems most fitting for the treatment of the question, to what extent, and in what manner, may conjectural criticism be safely exercised? For the last twenty years the text of Shakespeare has been subjected to a process, which for its wholesale destructiveness and the arrogance of its pretensions is wholly without parallel. The English press has teemed with works, from Mr J. P. Collier's pseudo-antique Corrector down to the late Mr Staunton's papers 'On Unsuspected Corruptions in the Text of Shakespeare,' most of which, in our judgment, have achieved no other result than that of corrupting and beraying the ancient text. We allow that some of the conjectures thus put forth are invaluable, and certain other may be

entertained for careful consideration ; but the mass we
repudiate as impertinent and barbarous. We deny the
need of any wholesale change, and impute great ignorance to the assailants :—not to insist on matters of
taste, which it is proverbially difficult to make matters
of controversy. We are fully able to prove the strength
of our position, by showing that the passages attacked
are proof against innovation by the power of their own
sense. We say to the assailants, ' When you propose
an emendation, you are virtually affirming that the
passage under your censure is nonsense, or at least
deficient in point or force, or inappropriate to the
occasion. In every case, then, in which we show the
passage to be good sense, and sufficient for its place in
the text, though possibly its meaning may be veiled in
" an ancient weed," we are challenging you to confess
your own incompetence, and thus to pronounce your
own condemnation.' Now to do this at full length and
in complete detail would require the dimensions of a large
volume : to teach the general truth by the force of particular examples is all that we now propose to accom-
plish. We propose to exemplify the growth of the
written English language in relation to the text of Shakespeare : to point out the dangers incident to all tampering with special words and phrases in Shakespeare :
to examine and defend certain words and phrases which
have suffered the wrongs of so-called emendation ; and
finally to discuss the general subject of the emendation
of the text, and to adduce some examples of passages re-

stored through this means. Having accomplished this, we shall gladly leave the old text, with its legions of archaisms and corruptions, to the tender mercies of those critics whose object is to conserve what is sound and to restore what is corrupt, and not at all to improve what, to their imperfect judgment and limited knowledge, seems unsatisfactory. To the arbitration of such critics we submit the question, whether in any particular case a word or phrase which is intelligible to the well-informed reader, however strange or uncouth, does or does not fulfil the utmost requirements of the cultivated mind, regard being had to the context, the situation, and the speaker.

CHAPTER I.

ON THE GROWTH OF THE ENGLISH LANGUAGE IN RELATION TO THE TEXT OF SHAKESPEARE.

REAT is the mystery of archaic spelling. Let us consider a few caprices of spelling, before proceeding to notice the vitality and consequent instability of written words: just as we must consider the symbolizing and uses of words before the grammatical structure and force of phrases. The word (σῆμα), rightly regarded, is an expressed *ens rationis*. It is purely a matter of convenience, whether it shall be represented to the eye or to the ear. We hold those to be in the wrong who would wholly subordinate the written sign to the sound, as if writing were essentially, as it is historically, a secondary process; and herein we dissent from the teaching of thorough-going Phoneticians. Be that as it may, the object of writing and speaking is not to *impart* the inner word (νόημα): for transmission of aught from one man's mind to another is impossible: but to *suggest* it. Still, in effect, something is communicated, or made common to both minds. In order that we may suggest to another man's mind any word that is in our own, we employ a medium which will stand for it, and lead him to understand it as we do. The written word is simply such a mediatorial symbol. The letters which constitute it are used to represent vocal sounds; and these may be of very variable force and range, while the **word** so symbolized is invariable. Thus *ea* and *a*, or *ea* and *e*, may by agreement represent the same vowel-sound; and *j* and *g*, or *j* and *i*, may, according to circumstances, stand for the same consonant-sound. But further, several written symbols that have little or nothing in common may stand for the same inner word : much more may **two** written symbols, which have grown by habit and custom from one spoken symbol, be regarded as equivalent forms of, or rather terms for, one and the same word. Thus, in the relative literature, we have *purture* and *pourtray*, *scase* and *scarce*, *scorce* and *scar*, *moe* and *more*, *windoe* and *windore*, *kele* and *cool*, *kill* and *quell*, *leese* and *lose*, *meve* and *move*, *cusse* and *kiss*, *make* and *mate*, &c. Not a shade of difference exists between the words in any of these pairs, unless, perhaps, in *scorce* and *scar*, the latter —and possibly not the former—having sometimes the sense of *value*, while both mean *barter*. Conversely several written symbols, which in the letter are identical, may not only stand for as many distinct words, but may be themselves also radically distinct. We have *must* (new wine), *must* (stale smell or taste), and *must* (il faut); *mere* (mare), *mere* (lake), and *mere* (pure); *sound* (sonus), *sound* (sanus, whole), *sound* (arm of the sea), a word possibly related to *swim*, or otherwise to *sunder*; *sound* (the swimming-bladder of the cod-fish), *sound* (sonder, to fathom), *sound* (swoon). These two classes of word-couples are not to be confounded with words which have only the same sound, without either similarity of sense or identity of spelling · e.g. *ought*, *aught*, and *ort* : nor yet with those which have only the same spelling, without either similarity of sense or identity of sound : e.g. *lead* or *tear*. The main points to keep distinctly in view in this study, are that the orthography of the written symbol, like its vocal expression, may change to almost any extent, and yet the internal word signified by such letters or sounds may remain unaltered ; and that the written or spoken symbol may remain unchanged, while the word signified changes, or that symbol may be used for words which have not a common origin

Shakespeare has had many ugly charges brought against him. Among others he has been arraigned for bad spelling and bad grammar ! But what Shakespeare's orthography was we have no certain means of knowing. If he had any system of spelling he was a century in advance of his contemporaries We have no knowledge beyond the capricious orthography of the compositors who printed his works. At the present day words are spelt according to a standard that is subject to only very slight variations. But even as late as the Commonwealth it may be truly affirmed that there was nothing like a standard. In the reigns of Elizabeth and James there was no attempt to ensure uniformity of spelling, nor is it likely that the writers or the readers of that time were conscious of any need or want in that respect. The question, what determined the orthography of the time, is exceedingly puzzling. We can here only record our growing conviction that silent reading was then much more than at present a purely mental process, and that the handwriters and printers of that day presented their readers with nothing incongruous or absurd when they indulged in the most outrageous versatility of literal construction. That *i* and *j*, or *u* and *v*, should have been regarded as identical consonants, or that *u* and *w*, or *i* and *y*, should have been regarded as identical vowels (though the least extraordinary of the many anomalies of their spelling), is quite enough to prove that readers were not fastidious on such points. One is sometimes disposed to wonder whether particular provinces had not, somewhat earlier, their conventional forms of spelling peculiarly adapted to the pronunciation prevalent in each province, and that these had become at length confusedly intermingled through the practice of engaging handwriters and compositors of various provinces to do the work of one establishment. There were, indeed, in Shakespeare's day limits to their vagaries. So far as we have been able to settle the point, few words were allowed as many as a dozen different forms of spelling. The word which we write *swoon* (a fainting-fit, or to faint) is a very curious example of Protean versatility. In a Nominale MS. of the 15th century, edited by Mr Thomas Wright, F. S. A., the word is figured *swoyne.* Chaucer and Lord Bacon have it, *swonn* or *swonne.* In the State

Trials, 1388, it is *swoon*; and so we find it in Milton, Dryden, and all the moderns. But Fabyan, 1364, spells it *swown* or *swowne*, and Spenser, 1589, and Walkington, 1607, adopt the same orthography; North, Shakespeare, and sundry others give it *sound*; and in Richard Hyrde's translations it is generally *swone*!

Within an assignable limit for each word, we may rest assured that every compositor in a printing-house spelt pretty much as seemed good in his own eyes. That he had just set up a word in one literal form was, perhaps, a reason why he should, on its recurrence, spell it in some other way. The spelling of all words, in fact, like that of Sam Weller's surname, depended 'upon the taste and fancy of the writer' or of the printer; and just as pedants with us will sacrifice the exact render of their best thoughts in order to avoid the repetition of a word (of all pedantries the most contemptible and reprehensible), so did an Elizabethan compositor sacrifice a just and compendious form of spelling to his love of variety, and his contempt of uniformity. If he had set up *foorth*, *poore*, *woorse*, he would on the next occasion present these words in the more concise style, *forth*, *pore*, *worse*. If he had set up *brydde* for the feathered biped, that feat of 'composition' became, if anything, a reason for transposing the *r* and *y*; for omitting a *d*, or the final vowel, or both; or for substituting *i* for *y*, on the next occasion when he had to cope with that Protean customer. To have printed, 'Among the bryddes the blackbrydde hath the saddest coat, and the moaste

dulcate mellodie,' would have been an offence against
the established economy, which dictated as much pro-
digality as was consistent with convenience ; for apart
from custom, which always has more weight than it
deserves, the probability is that the compositor could not
have conformed to a standard of orthography (if such a
thing had ever occurred to him as desirable on other
grounds) without constant embarrassment and frequent
unsightliness in the make-up of his lines. Obviously,
poetical works, in which the lines do not run on and
may always be adjusted without dividing the final words,
did not impose on him the same limitations as prose
works. But even in the latter it does not always appear
that the caprices of spelling were due to the necessities
of the case ; as in the two following examples, taken from
Hyrde's translation of Vives' *Instruction of a Christian
Woman* (ed. 1592 ; sig. D 4) : the sense is unimport-
ant here :—

> and specially if there bee any long
> space betweene the hollydaies. For think
> not y^t holy daies be ordained of the church
> to play on,

Here it is plain that in the second line it would have
made no difference to the compositor had he set up
' holy daies ' as in the third line ; or in the third line
' hollydaies ' as in the second line. Here there was no
such necessity as, in a line a little higher on the page,
occasioned the composite form ' workingdaies,' instead of
' working daies,' which we find in an intermediate line
where there was room for the *lead* or the *hyphen*   In-

deed it is hard to imagine any reason for omitting the *l* in the second ' holy ' which did not equally apply to the first, unless, indeed, the translator intended to exhibit obtrusively the original sense of the compound word, as *sanctæ dies*. In a word, variety in spelling was not always due to the condition of making up the lines without unsightly breaks; but is, at least sometimes, referable to chance or to preference. Again, sig. G 4,

> Let her bee content with a maide not
> faire and wanton.   fayre,

Here ' fayre ' is the catch-word at the bottom of one page, and ' faire ' is the first word on the next page. So likewise in Edward Phillips' *Theatrum Poetarum*, 1675 (The Modern Poets, p. 34-5), we have

> being for great Invention and Poetic
> heighth   height

where ' height ' is the catch-word at the bottom of one page, and ' heighth ' the first word on the next page. Again in *The Two Angrie Women of Abington*, Mistress Barnes says.

> ' I am abasde, my sonne, by Gourseys wife.'

On which Philip exclaims,

> ' By Mistresse Goursie!'

How are we to account for the change of orthography in the second example from Vives, unless we suppose that the *y* was thought as good an *i* as *i* itself? How, in the other examples, for the omission of the *h* from the catch-word, and the change of *ey* into *ie*, unless the orthography was thought a matter of little, or at least of secondary, importance? That it was so is proved by the fact that *y* was commonly used for *i* in manuscript: *e.g.* in a letter from Sir Walter Cope to Viscount Cranborne, dated 1604, preserved at Hatfield House, Herts, we read: 'I have sent and bene all thys morning huntyng for players Juglers & Such kinde of Creaturs but *fynde* them harde to *finde*,' &c   Similarly, I doubt not *ll* was thought no worse than *l*, and *l* as good as *ll* in such a word as *holyday*, where the *o* was not made long as in *holy*: the ear being then, in most cases, the arbiter of spelling

In fairness it must be allowed that in some few printed books of the Elizabethan era some approach to uniformity of spelling is occasionally discernible; but there was nothing like a standard of spelling till nearly a century later   In the work from which we took the first two examples (book i. chapter 3), in the course of a single page *wool* is spelled *woll* and *wooll*; in the next page, *woolle*; in the next, *wolle*; but *wool* is only found in compounds; and *woole* not at all'

In order to bring these remarks to a focus, in applying them to Shakespeare's text, let us confine ourselves to words of one initial letter, say H.   In Lupton's 'Too Good to be True,' 1580, *hair* is spelled twice *haire*, and once *heare*.   It is also spelled *heare* in Kyngesmyll's *Comforts in Afflictions*, 1585.   The latter is the less usual form.   It occurs, however, in earlier books than those.   It is used, for instance, in Drant's translation of

'Horace's Satyres,' 1566 ; where we read, 'I have shaved of his *heare :*' as to which passage it must be noted that *of* and *off* (like *to* and *too*, *on* and *one*, *the* and *thee*) are not always distinguishable in this literature, save by means of the context. Accordingly the participial adjective *haired*, being written and printed *heared*, *hear'd*, and *heard*, is sometimes presented in a form identical with the past participle of *hear* (audire). Here is an example from Shakespeare's *King John*, v. 2 :

> This un-heard sawcinesse and boyish Troopes,
> The king doth smile at.

where 'un-heard sawcinesse' is the sauciness of those striplings whose faces are hairless, and 'whose chins are not yet fledg'd' (2 Hen. IV., i. 2). Theobald, who must have been ignorant of the fact that *unheard* was merely *unhair'd* under an earlier orthography, proposed *unhair'd* as an emendation. This is merely an example of those orthographies, so fertile in confusion and mistake, which coincide where they should diverge, and diverge where they should coincide. Wickliff spelt *hard* (durus) *herd*, both forms being a departure from the A. S. *heard*. The Elizabethans, who inherited and retained the former style, spelt *herd* (armentum) *heard ;* and *heard* (auditus) *hard ;* and this last they pronounced as we do *hard* (durus) ; a fashion which is presupposed in *The Taming of the Shrew*, ii. 1 :

> Well have you *heard*, but something *hard* of hearing !

and in parts of Cambridgeshire and Suffolk we may still hear the same pronunciation.

Accordingly, those who would **contend** that these various forms of spelling afford evidence **of a rude** attempt at discrimination and *perseverance*, must needs admit that the attempt was wholly abortive; for what was gained by distinguishing *heard*, *hard* (auditus) from *heard* (conatus), was lost by confounding it with *hard* (durus); and what was gained by distinguishing *hard*, *heard* (armentum) from *herd* (durus), was **lost by confounding** it with *heard* (auditus).

Heard (armentum) occurs in *Coriolanus* i. 4, where it has been the occasion of an emendation.

> Enter Martius, cursing.
> All the contagion of the South light on you,
> You shames of Rome: you Heard of Byles and Plagues
> Plaister you ore, that you may be abhorr'd
> Farther than seene, and one infect another
> Against the Winde a mile: you Soules of Geese,
> That beare the shapes of men, &c.

The Johnsonian editors read, after Johnson himself,

> you herd of——Boils and plagues
> Plaster you o'er, &c.,

making a break after ' of,' as if the violence of Martius' passion left him no time to complete his abusive epithet, through the urgency of the imprecation. From Johnson to Collier every editor understands by *Heard*, armentum, save the latter, who reads ' unheard-of ' for ' a herd of : ' a conjecture which, like so many other candidates for admission into the text, is good *per se* as a probable

misprint, but bad in this place as a substitute for the
suspected words. The reason is this. Passion takes concrete forms, and avoids generalities. Martius would, in
the hands of a master, have been made to denounce a
specific malady on the Romans, rather than have weakened
the force of his substantives by the prefix ' unheard-of.'
But there is yet another reason. We cannot part with
Heard in the sense of armentum. Twice in this play the
people are so designated, and once in *Julius Cæsar :* in all
with the same contemptuous usage as in the passage under
consideration. We adduce this passage, not because the
difficulty admits of removal, but because it does not. It
is just one of those which we must be content to take
and leave as we find it. A score of suppositions may be
made to account for the presence of the preposition ' of.'
We might treat that preposition as governing ' boils
and plagues,' with the sense of *with ;* or as governed by
' you herd,' followed by an aposiopesis : or we might
make ' of' an adverb, equivalent to ' off !' and so forth :
all these expedients being about equally unsatisfactory ;
and there are still other possibilities to consider. But in
such a case it is not decision that is required, but faith.
We must stand by the text, and wait.

In a similar manner the male deer was symbolized
by *hart* and *hert ;* but our *heart* (cor) was generally spelt
hart, and still earlier *hert,* so that the alternative was no
security against confusion.

The passage quoted from *Coriolanus* resembles one in
Timon of Athens, Act iii. last Scene :

> Of man and beast the infinite malady
> Crust you quite o'er!

and it might be thought that the latter would be of service in construing or correcting the former. This led our friend Mr Perkins-Ireland of Knowe-Ware to propose a new expedient for restoring the passage in *Coriolanus;* viz. the supposition that a line is lost! He would read:

> You shames of Rome! you herd of . . . .
> An infinite malady of boils and plagues
> Plaster you o'er, &c.

He argues that the compositor's eye wandered from 'of' in the first line to 'of' in the second, whereby he omitted the first words of that line; and he supposes that the dotted portion was originally furnished with such words as 'timorous deer,' or 'heartless hinds.' All which we must allow to be very ingenious. But to such a method of dealing with a line which is *certainly* corrupt—and the one under consideration is far from being that—there is one serious objection, viz. that the supplied portions rest on no evidence whatever, presenting but one out of a great many equally plausible shifts. If, however, it be argued that such phrases as 'infinite malady,' 'timorous deer,' &c., are more likely to be the missing words, because they are used elsewhere by Shakespeare, it is sufficient to reply, that is a strong argument against them: e. g. forasmuch as 'infinite malady' is used in *Timon of Athens* in a precisely similar passage, it is most improbable that Shakespeare would have employed that phrase in *Coriolanus.* It will be helpful to know that Shakespeare's text cannot be emended in this fashion; for he never repeats himself in repeating the same thought or sentiment.[*]

To return from this digression: *help* and *heal* (or *hele*), though two distinct words, must, ages ago, have had a common origin, and are often used by Elizabethan writers indifferently. Thus, in *Phioravante's Secrets*, 1582, the second chapter is headed thus: 'To helpe the Falling Sicknesse in yong children.' But in the table of contents the same chapter is referred to as having the title, 'To heale the Falling Sicknes:' thus showing that one and the same sense was attached to both verbs. This use is common enough in Shakespeare:

> Love doth to her eyes repair
> To *help* him of his blindness,
> And being *helpt* inhabits there. —
>
> > *Two Gent. of Verona*, iv. 2

a conceit frequently found in the writers of this time, but never more beautifully expressed than here. Again,

> Not *helping*, death's my fee,
> But if I *help*, what do you promise me? —
>
> > *All's Well that Ends Well*, i. 2.

> though what it doth impart
> *Help* not at all, but only ease the heart.—*Rich. III.*, iv. 4.
> Turn giddy and be *holpe* by backward turning.—*Romeo and Juliet*, i. 2.

Helena, in *All's Well that Ends Well*, undertook, not what we mean by help, but the perfect cure of the King. We take one example from Milton:

---

[*] Our friend, seeing this in proof, indignantly disclaims the intention to affirm that the missing words in the second line were, *totidem verbis*, 'an infinite malady'; but he does not tell us what the exact words were. Why augment the mass of indefinite conjectures?

> *Helping* all urchin blasts, and ill-luck signs
> That the shrewd meddling elfe delights to make,
> Which she with precious vial'd liquors *heals.*—*Comus.* 845-7.

and yet one from Dr John Hall's *Select Observations upon English Bodies*, 1657 (translated by James Cook),

> and so she was suddenly *helpt*, p. 223.

That this means perfectly cured is shown by his habit of concluding his successful cases in this fashion: 'and so was cured,' p. 176, 'and in a short time became well,' p. 207, 'by which he was wholly delivered,' p. 238. Here, then, we have *help*, *cure*, *deliver*, used synonymously.

It is remarkable that this sense of *help*, used by every old English writer on Medicine, should have been unknown to the commentators on Shakespeare. Yet unknown to them it must have been; for otherwise they would not have proposed the emendation of the word in some half-dozen passages which almost force upon it the medical sense. Let us briefly consider these. In the *Comedy of Errors*, i. 1, the word occurs twice in one line:

> To seek thy *help* by beneficial *help*.

Though the custom of using the same word in different senses twice in one line, or even twice in contiguous lines, is not to be commended, it was common at that day. A better example of this could not be found than the line just quoted, or one in *Macbeth*, v. 3,

> Cleanse the *stuff'd* bosom of that perilous *stuff*,

or one in *K. Henry V.*, v. 1 :

To England will I *steal*, and there I'll *steal*.

The late Rev. A. Dyce (*A Few Notes on Shakespeare*,
1853, p. 129) gives a large collection of instances : and a
further instalment is contributed by Mr Marsh, in his
Lectures on the English Language, Lect. xxv. We have
given a few more in a foot-note.¹ Such instances must
not be confounded with those which constitute Section
xliii. of the late W. Sidney Walker's *Critical Exam. of*

---

the Text of Shakespeare, 1860, i. p. 276. In the face of so large an induction one would think that no critic of judgment would venture on emendation in the passage from the *Comedy of Errors*. It must be taken that the first *help* means *deliverance*, the second, *succour*. Yet the line has been tampered with by Pope, Steevens, Jackson, Collier, Singer, and Brae. We spare our readers an account of the *nostrums* of the first five. Mr A. E. Brae, in his admirable tract, entitled *Collier*,

---

Haply that name of chaste unhapp'ly set
This bateless edge on his keen appetite.—*Lucrece.*

Lean penury within his pen doth dwell,
That to his subject lends not some small glory.—*Sonnet* 84.

This mist, my friend, is mystical.—*Arden of Feversham.*

I sweare, Aurora, by thy starrie eyes,
And by those golden lockes, whose locke none slips.—
Stirling's *Aurora*, Sonnet x.

Still finest wits are stilling Venus' rose.—
Southwell's *Saint Peter's Complaint.*

I should leave grazing, were I of your flock,
And only live by gazing.—*Winter's Tale*, iv. 3.

Since we have locks to safeguard necessaries,
And pretty traps to catch the petty thieves.—*Hen. V.*, i. 2.

Me as his abject object, his eye revil'd.—*Hen. VIII.*, i. 1.

My Amen to't. All men's.—*Hen. VIII.*, iii 2.

Affection is a coal that must be cool'd.—*Venus and Adonis*

Making their tomb the womb wherein they grew —*Sonnet* 86.

That we may praise them, or themselves prize you.—
Herrick. *To Mildmay, Earl of Warwick.*

Coleridge, and Shakespeare, 1861 (pp. 75 and 150), discerning with his usual penetration the sense which the passage ought to carry, proposed to substitute *hele* for the first *help*, which would be acceptable enough, but for the fact that *help* means *hele* (*heal*) already. It is somewhat curious that *helpful* and *healthful* occur before, in the same sense; and that Rowe changed the first into *helpless;* and the editor of the Folio 1632 changed the second into *helpful:* so great a fatality seems to have invested this family of words, all occurring in one scene! Why ' *hapless* Ægeon ' was not converted by some one into ' *hopeless* Ægeon', and *hopeless* (on its first or second occurrence in that scene) was not converted into *hapless,* may well excite our wonder; that they escaped, our gratitude !

In 2 *Hen. IV.,* v. 4, *help* again occurs, and is again supplanted. Lord Say thus pleads his cause with Jack Cade :

> Long sitting to determine poor man's causes
> Hath made me full of sickness and diseases.

To which Cade replies, ' Ye shall have hempen candle then, and the *helpe* of hatchet.' Better sense could not be wished : nor do we see how it could be improved in any respect. Cade promises that his Lordship's diseases shall be administered-to ; he shall have hemp-candle and hatchet-cure : and if it be thought that Cade's small wit intended a poor quibble here, here it may be found for the seeking ; *cord* may be suspected under *candle,* and *helce* under *helpe,* with a side-glance at the saying 'to throw the helve after the hatchet.' But there is no occasion for this refinement of jest to be found in the passage. Now let us see what the critics have said about it. Farmer, with an eye to the latter pun, proposed to read *pap* for *help,* and adopts 'of *a* hatchet' from the Folio 1632; which reading Steevens and Ritson admiringly approve, the former saying, 'The help of a hatchet is little better than nonsense.' But the sense, notwithstanding, is perfect. Cade proposed to cure Lord Say's sicknesses by the aid of 'the sure physician death', by giving him the rope or the axe. The article inserted by the editor of the second Folio is an impertinence. In the CLIII. *Sonnet,* we have :

> I, sick withal, the *help of bath* desired.

How poor were the sound had he written, 'the help of a bath.' He meant there bath-cure : so in the former case he meant hatchet-cure. Finally, Mr A. E. Brae (in the work lately cited, p. 150) proposed to substitute *hele* for *help* in this place also. *Pap, helve,* and *hele* agree in this : they carry double : each may refer to a part of the hatchet, as well as to Lord Say's regimen. But they also agree in being impertinent, inasmuch as *help* in the sense of *healing* is a perfectly satisfactory reading.

The fatality spoken of is not confined to the *Comedy of Errors,* and 2 *Henry IV.* In *All's Well that Ends Well,* i. 3, we read,

> He and his physicians
> Are of a mind ; he, that they cannot *help* him,
> They, that they cannot *help.*

W. Sidney Walter suggests (with considerable doubt, however,) that *heal* should supersede the second *help;* and the late Mr Samuel Bailey, in contravention of a recognised and accepted canon, would abolish it in favour of *cure!* Once again in 2 *Henry VI.*, ii. 1, we have :

> Come, offer at my shrine, and I will *help* thee ;

where both Walker and Bailey read *heal* for *help*.

CHAPTER II.

IT will be perceived that *help*, and *heal*, or *health*, are not mere alternative forms of spelling one word; that in fact we have passed from the case of two such forms to that in which the orthographies belong to two words, coincident in one, at least, of their several significations. *Help* and *heal* are twins, separable as distinct words, yet having the features of a common parent. In Shakespeare we find *bleak* and *bleat* (balare); *break* and *breach* (ruptio); *make* and *mate* (consors); *plait* and *pleach* (intextus); and in other writers *attach* and *attack* (manum inicere); *bak* and *bat* (vespertilio), *moke, mote*, and *moth* (blatta); *quilk* and *quilt* (culcita); *reckless* and *retchless* (temerarius), where each pair or set of symbols are equivalents of one and the same word. But words which had once a strictly equivalent usage sometimes grow into synonyms having differences, or even to become the signs of distinct words: e.g *bleak, black,* and *bleach ; dole* and *deal ; list* and *lust ; marrow* and *marry,* &c. ; to which with qualification may be added such pairs or sets of

3

words as *wake*, *watch*, and *wait*; *ward* and *guard*, &c. Then, to crown the work, they may receive some modification of form by association with cognate, or even incognate signs. In this way is the balance of change maintained; for otherwise the loss, through the inaccurate or careless use of words, would soon enfeeble and debase the language to such an extent, that its literature would come to an end, through failure of the very means of expression.

Such considerations, with a multitude of others which we cannot set forth in this essay, are of the greatest importance in the criticism of the text of Shakespeare, particularly where we have to determine whether a word be interpretable as it stands, or a corruption demanding emendation.

The risk of applying conjectural criticism to the STILL LION increases as we proceed with our subject. Under apparently nonsensical words and phrases often lurk a sense and intelligence the most 'express and admirable.' Scarcely a year passes over our heads but new light, radiating from Elizabethan lore, shines into some 'dark passage' which the commentator with his 'farthing candle' has carefully shunned, or the conjectural critic, with his ingenuity and felicity, has tinkered again and again, and still in vain. An old author, writing of the latter, says, ' Hee is the Surgeon of old Authors, and heales the wounds of dust and ignorance ' (*Micro-Cosmographie*, 1628, § 35). If he did, it would be hard to denounce him for probing them. The complant, however, is just this, that he does not heal them. His surgery not unfrequently is butchery, but of the healing art he knows as little as a barber-surgeon. There is an old 'jeast' of such a one who, having to shave a customer, fell to cursing, because he cut his thumb, which he had put in his patient's cheek to force it out tense and firm. Happily Shakespearian barber-surgeons sometimes do this too, and, sadder or wiser by experience, handle their author with more feeling for the future, or leave him alone. But though some notable cures have been performed, notwithstanding, by the regulars of criticism; there yet remain, after all, a number of corrupt places which have persistently failed to profit by the expurgation of criticism. Of single words thus situated there are some thirty which thus get referred to the category of *immortal nonsense.* These, like the finest passages in Shakespeare, receive their share of homage.

First, as to textual difficulties affecting single words. Here are a sheaf of these 'ugly customers,' with most of whom every conscientious editor has had a mortal struggle, in which he was usually defeated.

An-heires. Merry Wives of Windsor, ii. 1.

Arm-gaunt. Antony and Cleopatra, i. 5.

Aroint. Macbeth, i. 3. Lear, iii. 4.

Barlet. Macbeth, i. 6.

Bone Timon of Athens, iii. 5.

Charge-house. Love's Labours Lost, v. 1.

Cars. Twelfth Night, ii. 5.

Cyme. Macbeth, v. 3.

Duedame. As You Like It. ii. 5.

Duug. Antony and Cleopatra, v. 2.

Empirickqutick Coriolanus, ii. 1

Esil. Hamlet.	*Seamels.* Tempest, ii. 1.
Land-damn. Winter's Tale. ii. 1.	*Skains-mates.* Romeo and Juliet,
Oneyers. 1 Hen. IV., ii. 1.	ii. 4.
Paiocke. Hamlet, iii. 2.	*Strachy.* Twelfth Night, ii. 5.
Prenzie. Measure for Measure,	*Vllorxa.* Timon of Athens, iii.
iii. 1	4.
Runaways. Romeo and Juliet, iii. 2.	*Vaughan.* Hamlet, v. 1.

From the penultimate word we will call the entire class *Ullorxals.*

We must allow, at the outset, that few of these strange words are utterly hopeless ; that one or two will trouble no one's peace any longer ; and that some bid fair to justify themselves, or to reveal, through their corruption, the true words which, owing to the blunder of reader, writer, or compositor, suffered this perversion. One can hardly doubt that *aroint* is a true word, though it has been often attacked and defended with great pertinacity, ingenuity, and learning. But, though a true word, its exact sense or root-meaning has not been ascertained. It has been thought to mean, *be off,* from the A. S. : and either *get thee behind,* or *break thy back,* from the French. But anyhow, the phrase, *rynt thee,* occurs in an old proverb.[*] *Barlet* was corrected by the editor of the folio 1632 ; it is a press-error for *martlet. Cyme* seems to be a misprint for *cené,* an obsolete form of *senna. Arm-gaunt* is assuredly a misprint ; for if such

---

[*] Mrs Browning has,

'Whisker'd cats *arointed* thee,'

and we observe in the *Animal World,* vol. v., p. 23.

'What wonder that the vermin fled *arointed.*'

a word was ever applied to a horse in the sense of *gaunt in the forequarters*, such a horse would be in Shakespeare's phrase, *shoulder-shotten* : and most certainly Antony's high-bred charger could not have been that   Surely *arrogant, rampaunt*, or *tarmagaunt* is a more likely correction than *arm-girt*, which has been confidently proposed : but *nostro judicio, termagant* would be a poor, if not an inappropriate epithet for the charger.   *Charge-house* is, almost certainly, *Church-house*, and the mis-spelling may be intentional to indicate the pronunciation, just as, in *Much Ado About Nothing*, Dogberry's *losses* may have been intended for *law-suits*.   On the other hand, was there ever such a word as *charge house*, for *domus curationis?*   *Scamels* has hitherto presented an irreducible crux, and ten substitutes for it have been proposed.   But we are happy to be able to state that at length it has proved its title to its prescriptive place in the text.   In Norfolk, a *scamel* is the name for the female *pick :* this being the male of *Limosa rufa*, or the Bar-tailed Godwit. (See Stevenson's *Birds of Norfolk*, vol. ii. p. 260.)   Still, we are not aware of such birds frequenting the rocks for breeding.   *Esil* is either *Eysell* (i.e. vinegar, or wormwood-wine), or the name of a Danish river (*Yssel*).   *Bone*, one of the most senseless corruptions in all Shakespeare, escaped unchallenged, strange to say, till Mr Staunton made two guesses at it in his edition of Shakespeare. It appears to be a misprint for *bed*, the termination *one* (instead of *ed*) having been caught from *onely* or from *none* in the same line.   Assuredly it was *there*, and there

only, that Alcibiades would have wished to prolong the
lives of the senators, who were already prepared by their
servile imbecility for being put away out of sight. Of
runaways we shall have somewhat to say hereafter.
Guesses enow have been made at the words for which
the rest in our sheaf may have been press-errors : but
with the exception of *Empirickqutick, skains-mates,*
and *Vaughan,* they all remain to this day shrouded in
hopeless obscurity. As to these three, *Vaughan* may
be a proper-name ; and if such a name be not found
in records of the time, it may well be a misprint for
Vaughan : which would be the tapster's name. *Skain,*
Mr Staunton tells us, used to be heard in the Isle of
Thanet, in the sense of scapegrace : but we do not
agree with him that this fact removes all difficulty
with the word. *Empirickqutick* till the advent of
the Perkins-imposture, was always turned into *empiric*
or *empirick,* and, we think, rightly so. It seems clear
that *Empirickqutick* belongs to a very definite class
of misprints, which we may call *duplicative.* Here
are a few examples of the class, observed by the
writer : — *Respectiveclive* for *respective,* in the office-copy
of a will : *axiomomata* for *axiomata,* in Whewell's *Philosophy of Discovery,* 1860, p. 144 : *puritie* for *pucitie,*
in the first folio of Shakespeare. And still more to the
purpose is the following : 'the whiche * * they ad-
judged for *pronostiquykys* and tokens of the Kynges
deth :' in Fabyan's *Chronicle,* vol. i. c. 246 : where the
word *pronostiquykys* is a misprint for *pronostiques.* This

is an error of near kin to *Empirickqutick*; and exempli-
fies the tendency of writers and compositors to repeat
some syllable in a word which is susceptible of two forms
of spelling: as, in this case, with a *qu*, or a *ck*. In practice we have often found ourselves anticipating the term-
inal consonants of the next word, in the one we happened
to be writing: as *make work* for *may work*; *make speak*
for *may speak*; and so forth: and in the first edition of
The Still Lion, at p. 209 of the *Jahrbuch*, the former
error of writing was actually made in the copy, and set
up, without being subsequently detected: whereby a
second misprint was grafted upon a line in the *Tempest*,
as if in compensation for losing the one we had it in
hand to expose and correct. So it came to pass that the
very page containing our remarks on duplicative errors,
presented an example of the very kind. Of the residue of
the words in our sheaf, all of which are mere printer's
sphinx-riddles, *duedame* (which, like *aroint* and *prenzie*,
has the distinguished honour of occurring several times
in the text of Shakespeare) has been regarded as a
nonsensical refrain; and in support of that view Mr J.
O. Phillips (Halliwell) cites, from the burden of an old
song, *dusadam-me-me*. But such refrains are common
enough; and if one could only be sure that *duedame* is
no more than *such* a refrain, one would not be solicitous
about its pedigree. Allowing it to be such a refrain,
and therefore one in which no meaning would be looked
for, is it likely that Amiens would have been made to
show such solicitude about it? Had it been, for instance,

dan-dyry-cum-dan, thrice repeated, would Shakespeare have made him ask Jacques, 'What's that *dan-dyry-cum-dan?*' Surely not.

To conclude this chapter, we add five petty Ullorx-als, which demand and admit of a simple remedy:

'*meant* damnable.'——*All's Well that Ends Well*, iv. 3: read, with Hanmer, *most* (moast).

'*path* thy native semblance on.'——*Julius Cæsar*, ii. 1: read, with Coleridge, *pat*.

'As thick as *tale*.'——*Macbeth*, i. 3: read, with Rowe, *hail*.

'*pith* and moment.'　　　　　　) *Hamlet*, iii. 1
'When our deep plots do *pall*.')　　and v. 2: read, with the 4tos, *pitch* and *fall*.

CHAPTER III.

ON THE DIFFICULT PHRASES IN SHAKESPEARE, AND THE DANGER OF TAMPERING WITH THEM.

UT the critic is in danger of assuming, on insufficient evidence, that not a word only, but an entire sentence, owes its obscurity to the corruption of words by scribes and printers. It is convenient to consider phrases under three heads: *idioms, idiotisms,* and *idiasms:* which may be briefly explained as follows :—

All living languages are in a state of continuous change. Not only do words fall into disuse, and others accrue to the general stock, not only do the orthographical forms in which they are presented to the eye undergo change, but each several word is ever more or less changing its meaning, both in scope and in force. Some words (like *shy, secure*) obtain a signification directly contrary to their former meaning ; or (like *let, prevent*) retain two contrary meanings at once. Others (like *knave, piece, lewd*) pass from a respectable to a disreputable sense : while others (like *liberty, practice,* *occupy,*[*] *convey*) throw off their disreputable association, and become honourable symbols of speech. The literal sense of some gives way to the figurative, and, perhaps more rarely, the reverse; and a word which has done duty as one part of speech becomes another. But not only do words thus change; but all kinds of expression written and spoken change also. The normal affinities of parts of speech constitute the *idiom*: the singular phrase, which does not conform to the idiomatic construction, is the *idiotism*. There remain phrases and words peculiar to some creative writer; these we call *idiasms* (ἰδιασμοί). Thus it appears that the *idiom* is a regular, the *idiotism* a proverbial, and the *idiasm* a private and peculiar mode of phraseology. At present we shall confine our remarks to complete sentences, and the changes and corruptions of sentences; passing by that intermediate class of corruptions which involve several words, but not an entire phrase.

The idioms of a language change, but slowly, under dialectical and colloquial influences; and apart from those influences, scarcely change at all. But idiotisms are constantly slipping out as pedantries, and creeping in as slang. Shakespeare's works, like all the literature of his day, as might be expected, contain many idioms which by this time have become obsolete or dead. The worst of it is, that we read him so much, and with so

---

[*] ' A captain! These villains will make the word "captain" as odious as the word "occupy", which was an excellent good word before it was ill-sorted.'—2 *Hen. IV.*, ii. 4. This word is now restored to its old respectability.

little appropriate knowledge and steady reflection, that we get habituated to the look and sound of his phraseology, and come at last to think we understand it, mistaking the familiar for the intelligible. The same has come to pass of the Authorised Version of the Holy Scriptures. Such an idiom as is involved in the sentence, 'I do the [thee] to wytene [understand] that it is made be [by] enchauntement,' in Maundevile's *Voiage and Travaile* (A.D. 1322-46), is as dead as a door-nail: yet we have the same, 'We do you to wit of the grace of God,' in the A. V.; and we read this over and over again, and get so used to it, that it comes upon us as the voice of an old familiar friend, while it is as unintelligible as an unknown tongue, and was obsolescent when King James' Bible was first printed. How often, too, have we read the lines in *Hamlet*, v. 2,

Does it not, think thee, stand me now upon,
  * * * * is't not perfect conscience,
To quit him with this arm?

but to how many readers is this idiotism intelligible? For one thing, that passage is absurdly pointed in most editions of the play; the true construction being, that the idiotism in question governs the infinitive, 'To quit (requite) him with this arm.' The same expression is employed in three other places in Shakespeare: viz. *Rich. II* ii. 3; *Rich. III.* iv. 2; and *Antony and Cleopatra*, ii. 1. See also *Romeo and Juliet*, ii. 3 ('I stand on sudden haste'—but which is not *identical* with the expression in question). It is usually explained correctly in annotated editions; but the editors satisfy themselves by quoting from other parts of Shakespeare in illustration of it. We give two contemporary examples from other works

Then they are worthy to be hanged eternally in Hel, that will not most gladly, ＊ ＊ ＊ come to heare the eternall God the King of heaven himselfe speake, who doth pronounce, &c., &c. . . . which to heare, marke, remember, and observe, *it stands us upon*.—Lupton's *Too good to be true*, 1580, p. 25.

It was concealed, and therefore *stands upon*,
Whether through our advice you will be saved,
Or in his beastly entrails be en-graved.
Cupid and Psyche, by Shakerley Marmion, 1637.

Again, how often have we read that inimitable scene in 2 *Hen. IV.* i. 2, where Falstaff says of his mercer,

A whoreson Achitophel! a rascally yea-forsooth knave! *to bear* a gentleman *in hand*, and then stand upon security.

This idiotism also occurs in six other places in Shakespeare: viz. *The Taming of the Shrew*, iv. 2; *Much Ado About Nothing*, iv. 1.; *Measure for Measure*, i. 5; *Cymbeline*, v. 5; *Macbeth*, iii. 1; *Hamlet*, ii. 2. Examples of this are commoner in Elizabethan literature, than of the former. Here are five:

There be many diseases in the bodies of men and beasts which he [the Devil] seeth will breake foorth unto lamenesse or unto death, he *beareth* the Witches *in hand* he doth them.
Giffard's *Dialogue Concerning Witches and Witchcraft*, 1603. Ep.

And yet much worse is it to make them to mary by striving and hate, threatning, and sute: as when they goe to lawe together, the man for the woman, *bearing* her *in hand* that shee is his wife :—Vives' *Instruction of a Christian Woman* (R. Hyrd), 1592. Sig. N 2.

And as for the manner of his Apostacy or backsliding, the priest himselfe, nay the partie himselfe, nay we our selves know to be farre otherwise then they woulde faine here *beare* us *in hand*.—Raester, 1598, last page.

And againe, those which being hitherto *borne in hande* that men's soules returne againe on earth, * * * will confesse the like.— *Of Ghostes and Spirites*, 1596. To the Reader

Salomon teacheth us to chasten children with the rod, and so to make them stand in awe : he doth not say, we must *beare* them *in hand* they shall be devoured of Bugges, Hags of the night, and such like monsters. *Ibid.*, p. 21.

(It also occurs at pp. 27, 31, 32, 53, 187, 210, and 211 of this curious and instructive treatise, which is a translation of the well-known work, *De Lemuribus*, of Lavaterus ; and it is common in Ben Jonson, Heywood, and the early dramatists.) The phrase is of great antiquity. The earliest example that has come under our notice is in Drant's *Horace's Sat.* (Sig. A ii.) 1566, but is there in the form *to hold one in hand*, in the sense of *persuade*, simply As to the meaning of these idiotisms, *To stand upon* is to be incumbent on. *To bear in hand* is to inspire misplaced confidence or belief.

It were easy to multiply to any extent examples of obsolete idiotisms for further illustration take these four : *to die and live by a thing ; to remember one's courtesy ; to cry on a thing ; to cry game*, all of which have been mercilessly handled by the editors and commentators. In cases where a few examples of the phrase have been discovered in contemporary literature the love of emendation has yielded to the force of evidence

Where that evidence cannot be adduced the suspected phrase falls an easy prey to 'conjectural felicity,' i.e. to barbarous innovation.

The slow and comparatively slight changes which the true idioms of the language have undergone, do, in fact, occasion the critic no difficulty. The expression *No is?* (for *Is not?*), *No did? No have?* is a totally obsolete idiom ; one instance of which occurs in Shakespeare, viz. in *King John*, iv. 2, where 'No had' of the Folio has been usually altered into *Had none.* (See *Notes and Queries*, 1st S. vii. 520 & 593.) The use of the relative absolute (with active or neuter participles) was in use as late as Locke : at least three instances of it are in Shakespeare : viz. two in *The Tempest*, i. 2 (' *Who having*, &c., he did believe,' &c. ' A noble Neapolitan, &c., *who being*, &c., did give us '), and one in *Love's Labours Lost*, i. 1 (' *Who dazzling* so, that eye shall be,' &c.), in the first of which the seeming solecism has given occasion to several emendations. The suppression of the relative as subject was almost as normal a usage as its expression ; and in some half-dozen places in Shakespeare, where such is the construction, the text has been conjecturally altered. But above all other peculiarities of the Elizabethan idiom was that of inflectional conjugation, e.g. the use of the third person plural in *s* or *th*, which in the case of Shakespeare has been almost always regarded as a grammatical inaccuracy ! Some critics have gone so far as to reflect on Shakespeare's imperfect education, and to attempt the poor joke, that if, as Mr

Halliwell asserts, he did go to Stratford Grammar School, he must have learnt anything but grammar! Another explains the apparent irregularities in Shakespeare by the supposition that 'the thought blew the language to shivers', which, it appears, is a natural characteristic of literary Genius! Accordingly it has been deemed an act of kindness to cure him of those defects. So it has happened that the editors have corrected his grammar, as well as modernized his spelling; but in doing this they have betrayed an amount of ignorance for which they would not otherwise have had the discredit. THE STILL LION HAS BEEN AMPLY AVENGED ON HIS FOES.

After all that a sound knowledge of English Literature and of the evolution of the English Language, with the concurrence of conjectural skill, can effect in vindicating and restoring the genuine text of Shakespeare, there still remain a number of corruptions which, like the Ullorxals, are mere printers' Sphinx-riddles. These, however, unlike the Ullorxals, consist of several entire words, and are cases not so much of corrupt words as of corrupt phrases; and, while it is possible that some of these are pure idiasms, it is much more probable that they are idiotisms of the time or textual corruptions. Among this numerous family are the following, which will serve as samples of the class:

1.   I see that men make ropes in such a scarre
That we'll forsake ourselves.

All's Well that Ends Well, iv. 2.

2.   It is as lawful,
      For we would count give much to as violent thefts
      And rob in the behalf of charity.— *Troilus and Cressida*, v. 3.

3.   most monster-like, be shewn
      For poor'st diminutives, for dolts,
                                    Antony and Cleopatra, iv. 10.

4.   The dram of eale
      Doth all the noble substance of a doubt
      To his own scandal.—*Hamlet*, i. 4.

5.   That I had no angry wit to be a lord,
                                    Timon of Athens, i. 1.

6.   I would they would forget me, like the virtues
        Which our divines lose by 'em.—*Coriolanus* ii 3.

From the first of these examples, I call the family *Rope-scarres*. In dealing with these the success of the critic has been infinitesimally small. We are indebted to the collations in the Cambridge Edition of Shakespeare (supplemented by two conjectures, one by the late Rev. Dr Wellesley, and one by ourselves) for the numbers in the following table. If these numbers do not fairly represent the relative difficulty of these passages, they will at least testify to the absolute difficulty of all, and of the ill success that has rewarded criticism. It should be borne in mind here, that to the obscurity of the passage must be added the dulness of the critic. The difficulty may lie, as it often does in fact, as much in the perceptions of the recipient, as in the obscurity of the phraseology to be received.

1,	19 conjectures.		4,	40 conjectures.
2,	15	,,	5,	15	,,
3,	3	,,	6,	6	,,

It would be a thankless task to specify the actual number of Rope-scarres in the entire text of Shakespeare. The list is considerable: but to our mind, the wonder is that the text is, on the whole, so free from misprisions and dislocations. When we consider the misprints which disfigure modern books, even those which have received the most vigilant and jealous supervision, both of Editor and of Reader, it is to be expected that, at a time when printing was not conducted on so methodical a plan as at present, and when important works were generally issued without any regular editorial supervision, the first Edition of Shakespeare should exhibit a harvest of typographical casualties. On the whole we are disposed to regard that edition as being quite as free from typographical errors as the majority of dramatic works of that time. Moreover, we are convinced that much of the obstinate intractability of these Rope-scarres is due to the intermixture of obsolete phrases, Shakespearian idiasms, or forgotten allusions, with certain typographical errors; so that it is not surprising that the mere conjectural critic should find himself unable to set them right by the mere exercise of his ingenuity and taste.

CHAPTER IV.

AN EXAMINATION AND DEFENSE OF CERTAIN WORDS AND
PHRASES IN SHAKESPEARE, WHICH HAVE SUFFERED
THE WRONGS OF EMENDATION.

HE three foregoing chapters are intended rather
for warning than for the value of the criticisms
which they contain. Let us now apply ourselves to a selection of passages, which have received
the doubtful benefit of conjectural emendation. Our
warning has been somewhat prolix ; but our best excuse
will be found in the treatment to which portions of the
text of Shakespeare have been subjected at the hands of
his censors and critics. So capricious are the objections
preferred against particular words and phrases, that it is
a sheer impossibility to anticipate them. Accordingly
the antiquarian of the English Language, who essays the
vindication of the old text, labours under an immense dis-
advantage. To learn the acknowledged peculiarities and
difficulties of that text is a labour of love ; and to store
them up and retain all the salient points of Shakespeare's
phraseology in an ever ready and lively memory, is but
a light prelude to the business that is to follow. With

these matters ever consciously before him—' full of eyes before and behind '—the critic wades through a huge store of the literature of the 16th and 17th centuries, noting down every word, phrase, and allusion, which can by any possibility throw light on the text of his venerated author. This is the toil which has been achieved by all the leading editors from Steevens to Dyce, with a few exceptions, which it is as well to forget. Fit propædeutic is such a course of study and discipline to the more genial and graceful duties of verbal criticism! The labour achieved, the **preliminary** requirement complied with at the cost of much time and effort, some vain reader, of blissful ignorance but of lively fancy, conceives a liking for what he pleasantly regards as the *game* of criticism, and rushes into the columns of some periodical, such as the *Athenæum*, or *Notes and Queries*, to proclaim with flourish of trumpets a new reading. His conjecture is, as a matter of course, described as ' an undoubted restoration of a passage which has for two centuries and a half defied exposition or correction!' Then follows, equally as a matter of course, the discovery of a mare's nest. The would-be critic has mistaken the sense of a passage both well known and perfectly **understood**; whereupon he proposes what he takes for a new conjecture, but **which** in many cases is an old and not very creditable acquaintance, whose familiar features may be seen recorded in some *Variorum hortus siccus*, under the **sanction** of a venerable name. In a few of such cases it is no great tax on the antiquarian to produce his authority for adhering to the old text : but where there are so many ' Richmonds in the field ', one naturally and reasonably grudges the superfluous labour of vindicating what had never been injuriously assailed. He rightly feels that faith in the prodigious learning of a Walker or a Dyce is a simple duty with learners ; and that for them to put a word or phrase on its trial merely because they ' don't seem to see it ', is an impertinence, against which every well-informed and competent editor would jealously guard his columns. In some cases, however, the vindication of a challenged expression in Shakespeare is inconclusive, by reason of the very absurdity of the challenge. We have more than once seen an expression denounced as senseless, which assuredly had never occasioned the slightest difficulty with any one ; and for this very reason, no critic had ever thought it worth while to register the instances of its use which had occurred in the course of his reading. We ourselves have noticed a peculiarity of language occurring over and over again, of which we did not stop to record a single example, because its employment by Shakespeare had never provoked remark, and seemed unable to afford a foothold for suspicion. Yet we have lived to see the passage in which it occurred obelized as an ' unsuspected corruption ', and to find ourselves incapacitated, through the want of superhuman prescience, for the work of vindication. It is impossible to stop every cranny against the aggression of a misplaced ingenuity, which 'infects unseen', and corrupts the text it seems to restore

As the inquiry we are about to institute is 'of the dust dusty' in its extreme dryness and in the antiquity of the literature which will illustrate it, we will preface it with a couple of relevant anecdotes. As both are derived from the store of our forgetive friend Mr Perkins-Ireland, we will not vouch for their literal truth. He tells us that a literary bore of his acquaintance came to him one day with a pocket edition of Shakespeare, in which a well-known line in *King John* thus stood :

'Bell, Booke, and Candle shall not *course* me back.'

The bore was swelled with the importance of a critical discovery : his 'business looked out of him'. 'A restoration !' he triumphantly exclaimed, pointing to the line, in which over the antepenult he had written the word, *curse*. '*Course*,' said he decisively, 'is a misprint for *curse*.' Mr Perkins-Ireland was taken aback by the apparent felicity of the conjecture : but promptly asked his friend for his proofs. Thereupon the bore produced an extract from page 17 of Lupton's *Too good to be true* (an ominous title !), which ran thus :

'The best thing the Pope can do is to *curse* him out again, with Bel, Booke, and Candle.'

This he followed up with another from page 23 of *Ariosto's Seven Planets Governing Italie,*

> ' Then roares the bulles worse then the Basan host,
>   Whilst Belles and bookes and candles *curses* boast.'

This he was following up with others : when Mr Per-kins-Ireland stopped him, and pointed out that one thing was yet unproved, that *curse* was ever spelt *course*. The bore was indignant at so discomforting a requisition, which he naturally regarded as unreasonable : for if *course* was just *curse* under an archaic orthography, the credit to be awarded to the bore was of a very different kind, he thought of an inferior kind, to that he claimed : he would be no longer the emender, but the exponent of the word in the text. But whether he would or no, the thing was virtually done for him : for Mr Perkins-Ireland himself, found *course* spelt *curse* in Leland, *scourge* spelt *scurge* in Richard Hyrde, so he frankly owned that his friend had, at least, invested the passage in *King John* with a new and most admirable sense Their triumphal rejoicings, however, were of very short duration. Fortunately, before breaking up the confer-ence, Mr Perkins-Ireland, with his well-known caution, had the prudence to turn to his *Variorum*. There, to his and his friend's astonishment, he found the line in *King John* printed thus,

> ' Bell, Book and Candle shall not *drive* me back : '

and so it stood in half-a-dozen other editions at hand. Obviously his friend's pocket-edition was, at least in that line, misprinted ; and he departed chap-fallen at this new discovery, that he had been bringing his critical resources to bear on a word which was not in Shakespeare's text!

That's not a bad anecdote: but here's a better Both enforce the lesson, 'look before you leap'. It is as dangerous to criticize a passage without consulting the context, as it is to do so without verifying it. Mr Perkins-Ireland was the critic in this case. He was reading *Much Ado About Nothing*, ii. 1 (another ominous title!), when he came upon the passage,

'and then comes repentance, and, with his bad legs, falls into the cinque-pace faster and faster, till he sink [apace] into his grave.'

The addition of *apace* was made by his cousin, Mr Thomas Perkins, of Folio 1632 celebrity; and Mr Perkins-Ireland thought it eminently ingenious. 'But,' said he to himself, 'What is the meaning of *cinque-pace*? Surely it must be some sort of disease: in fact the whole passage reminds one of Falstaff's *degrees* of sickness and wickedness, which my cousin Thomas so rashly altered into *diseases*.' Thereupon he took down his copy of Andrew Boord's *Breviarie of Health*, and to his delight found a disease called the *Sinkopis*, the description of which accorded admirably with the description of Repentance 'with his bad legs', sinking into his grave It is not to be wondered at that he believed himself to have hit upon a capital emendation. But for all that his caution did not desert him; and he once more applied himself to the text, this time reading it with the context; and on perceiving that Beatrice had just said, 'Wooing, wedding, and repenting, is as a

Scotch jig, a measure, and a *cinque-pace*,' began to be ashamed of his precipitation, if not of his ingenuity. The fact is, that emendation is always a ticklish business. THE CRITIC CAN NEVER TELL WHETHER THE LION IS DEAD, ASLEEP, OR ONLY SHAMMING SLEEP. HE TAKES A DEAL OF WALKING-ROUND, AND TICKLING WITH A LONG STRAW, AND POKING WITH A STICK, BEFORE ONE CAN BE REASON-ABLY SURE THAT IT IS SAFE TO COME TO CLOSE QUARTERS WITH HIM.

We will now proceed to consider in detail a dozen selected characteristics of Shakespeare's text.

1. It is remarkable that it is not the most difficult passages in Shakespeare that have occasioned the greatest dispute: on the contrary, the most hotly con-tested questions relate to passages of which the only fault in the eyes of a competent critic is, that the sense is perhaps too obvious. No one, attentively considering such passages, can fail to find *some* sense, though per-haps every one feels that after all *the* sense intended by Shakespeare has eluded his vigilance, and believes that something better remains to be found *in* the text, or, failing that, to be found *for* it. In such speculation, whether of investigation or of tentative substitution, there is, on the whole, much good; provided the critic does not overlook what is ' under his nose', which is, in so many places, the very sense which ought to put a term to further speculation. Here is an example in point. Juliet, impatiently awaiting the advent of Romeo to her nuptial couch, thus invokes the Night,

> Spred thy close Curtaine Love-performing night,
> That run-awayes eyes may wincke, and *Romeo*
> Leape to these armes, untalkt of and unseene.
>
> *Romeo and Juliet*, iii. 2.

So the folio 1623, and two of the quarto editions, the two earlier quartos reading *runnawayes*. For this word *run-awayes*, which was not suspected till after Capell's Edition, and which admits of explanation without the least *tour de force*, we find that no less than thirty-two substitutes have been proposed, whereof seven have been inserted in the text of as many editions! As we do not intend to furnish a list of the conjectural readings for any other passage, we will do so in this case, merely to show with what fatuous imbecility the conjectural critics would fain over-ride the diction of Shakespeare, wherever it happens to be obscured by archaism or weakened by seeming platitude. First, however, we must premise that there was such a substantive as *runaway*, and that, in the language of the time, it was for the whole gamut of its meaning the same as *runagate*, with which every English Churchman is familiar from the version of the Psalms appended to the Liturgy. But when it is said that Jehovah 'letteth the *runagates* continue in scarceness', the persons who are so let to starve are *delinquents*, those who are *runaways* from duty, who habitually *run away* from or *desert* the cause they are bound to support. Golding thus employs both *runagates* and *runaways*, to describe those who have deserted the enemy's camp, and come over to Cæsar's. But the senses of *delinquent* and *deserter* are special senses both of *runagate* and of *run-away*. The more general signification of either word is, one who having treacherously acquired anything (news or goods), makes off with it, *runs away* to escape detection and appropriate what he has so obtained. In this sense Shakespeare may very well have used the word in *Romeo and Juliet*. But again, vagabonds who haunt the streets towards dusk for dishonest purposes might be very well called *runagates* or *runaways*. Or, once more, *runaways* may describe those who were hostile to the union of Romeo and Juliet, and who would not scruple to use any means to discover Romeo's intended visit, and to place obstacles in his way. It will be observed that the textual word 'run-awayes' may stand either for *runaways'* or for *runaway's*; and if satisfactory sense can be made of either, surely emendation is an impertinence. Mr N. J. Halpin, in a remarkable Essay printed among the *Shakespeare Society's Papers* and called 'The Bridal Runaway', has made out a very strong case for the latter form. taking Runaway as the epithalamial sobriquet of Love. But even if that view should be decided against, we have still the former, which, as we have shown, admits of ample justification. Our own impression is that Shakespeare is using the word as a plural possessive—*runaways' eyes*. He might, for the sense, have just as well have employed *runagates'*: but not for the verse, for though in *runagates'* he would preserve the symptosis of the *run* and *Rom*, he would lose that of the *ways'* and *wink*.

But not only is *runaways'* defensible, but it is easily shown to be the appropriate word for the place. Juliet says,

> Spred thy close Curtaine Love-performing night,
> That run-awayes eyes may winke,——

What eyes? To answer which question we must determine what eyes are made to wink, or are deprived of their function, *as a consequence* of the advent of Night. Shakespeare might have used a very reprehensible metaphor, and spoken of Day's *eyes*, as some of his contemporaries did: but the winking of Day's eyes, and the closure of Night's curtain, are one and the same thing, not distinct operations of which the one is dependent upon the other. So, despite Mr Dyce's deliverances, *those* eyes are excluded from the possibilities of the case. Shakespeare might also, and with great propriety, have spoken of Night's eyes, meaning the stars; but unless by *wink* he meant *twinkle*, the closure of Night's curtain, so far from being the condition upon which the stars are made to wink, or are veiled, is in fact the only occasion of their shining forth: so Night's eyes are equally excluded. Despite Walker and Mitford, no poet speaks of the Moon's *eyes;* but if Shakespeare had ever done so, he would not have done so here; for the advent of Night only serves to make her brighter. Lastly, can the eyes alluded to be those of either or both of the lovers. To answer this we must consider the next line:

> That runawayes eyes may winke, and *Romeo*
> Leape to these armes, untalkt of and unseene,

from which it appears that the winking of those eyes is
the condition precedent of Romeo's security from detection : and it would be an insult to common sense to
inquire whether the closing of Juliet's eyes, or of
Romeo's eyes, could contribute to that result. Similarly,
the twinkling of the stars, brought out by the approach
of night, could not help to ensure Romeo's immunity
from suspicion ; so that cannot be the winking contem-
plated by Shakespeare. We are thus driven into a
corner, and are obliged to find the objects connoted by
runaways in those who, but for the darkness, might spy
out the approach of the lover, and betray the secret to
parties interested in the frustration of his design ; or
even in those very parties themselves ; or in both : in a
word, we must understand by *runaways*, persons secretly
on the watch to thwart the assignation of the lovers.*

There is nothing unusual, recondite, or far-fetched,
in this explanation : yet the bulk of the critics will not
have it. Does it not make one blush for mortal dulness

---

* Mr F. J. Furnivall takes this view in a letter in the *Academy*
(March 21, 1874). After quoting *Fugitif, Roder, Rodeur*, &c. from
Cotgrave 1611, he concludes, "Shakspere's runawayes, runagates, or
runabouts, were the *rodeurs des rues* with a different object, men who'd
leave no young lovers 'untalkt of and unseene', while the light
lasted." But *roder les rues* he explains, after Cotgrave, to walk the
streets "especially at night, to *see* the town served." A *rodeur des
rues* then is the last person to allow a nocturnal assignation to elude
his vigilance. He at least is no winker.

that such a passage should have been singled out for almost exhaustive emendation? Perhaps the best way of presenting these conjectures is to classify them under the leading conceptions which gave them birth.

(1) It is conceived that *run-awayes* is a misprint for the proper name of the source or sources of daylight, moonlight, or starlight. Hence we are favoured with 5 conjectures: *Luna's*, Mitford: *Cynthia's*, Walker: *Uranus'*, Anon.: *Titan's*, Bullock: *wandering* (*wandering eyes* being the planets), (*Athenæum*, August 6, 1870).

(2) It is conceived that *run-awayes* is a misprint for some word of which the last syllable is *day's*. This gives us 4 more: *rude day's*, and *soon day's*, Dyce: *sunny day's*, Clarke: *noonday's*, Anon.

(3) It is conceived that *run-awayes* is a misprint for the name of a mythical person. This gives us 4 more: *th' Runaway's* (i. e. the Sun), Warburton: *the runaway's*, Capell: *Rumour's*, Heath: *Renomy's* (i. e. *Rénommée*), Mason.

(4) It is conceived that the first syllable of *run-awayes* is a misprint for *sun*. This gives us 4, one being already mentioned. *Sun away*, Taylor: *sun-awake's*, Brady: *sun-aweary*, McIlwaine · *sunny day's*, Clarke (as before).*

(5) It is conceived that the misprint is in the last syl-

---

* On seeing this proof Mr Perkins-Ireland maliciously asks whether any one has ever proposed to read *Grundy's eyes!*

lable only of *run-awayes*. This gives us 5 more *ranagate's*, Beckett *run-away*, Blackstone: *run-astray*, Taylor: *run-abouts'*, Keightley: *runaway spies*, H. K.

(6) It is conceived that *ware*, or *wary*, formed part of the word for which *run-awayes* stands. This gives us 3 more. *Unawares*, Jackson: *unwary*, Taylor: *waryones'*, Anon.

(7) A class to which we may assign various conjectures which do not fall in the other six. We have *rumorous* and *rumourers'*, Singer: *enemies*, Collier: *rouriage*, Dyce: *yonder*, Leo: *ribalds*, and *roaming*, Anon.: *Veronese* (*Nation*, May, 1871); amounting to 8 more :—

on which miscellaneous repast, of both the wholesome and the baneful, we may well ask one blessing—a speedy deliverance from one and all!

2. We sometimes meet with a conventional phrase or idiotism employed by Shakespeare in a sense peculiar to himself, i. e. as an idiasm. The following example is most instructive. We quote from *As You Like It*, iii. 5 (folio 1623)

> the common executioner
> Whose heart th' accustom'd sight of death makes hard,
> Falls not the axe upon the humbled neck,
> But first begs pardon : will you sterner be
> Then he that dies and lives by bloody drops?

The Cambridge Edition records nine monstrous substitutes for the phrase *dies and lives*. The simple fact is, that this phrase was a recognized *hysteron proteron*; and we are indebted to Mr R. W. Arrowsmith (*Notes and Queries*, 1st S. vii. 542) for a collection of early examples illustrating its use, which seem to have been entirely overlooked by all the previous editors and commentators. Mr Halliwell, in his Folio Edition, supplements Mr Arrowsmith's labours, but fails to recognize the fact that none of the examples adduced is precisely in point. That the phrase *to die and live* was formerly used for *to live and die*, is fairly established; but of the phrase *to die and live by a thing* not a single example has been adduced. Mr Arrowsmith tells us that *to die and live* means 'to subsist from the cradle to the grave'. Shakespeare's executioner, then, must have been initiated into his 'mystery' pretty early. But one of Mr Arrowsmith's examples is from a work now before us, '*The Pilgrimage of Kings and Princes:*' at page 29 of which we read, 'Behold how ready we are, how willingly the women of Sparta will *die and live* with their husbands.' So that we are gravely asked to believe that, according to this old writer, the Spartan women were so precocious that they 'subsisted' with their husbands 'from the cradle to the grave!' Hitherto, then, no example in point has been discovered. But even if the phrase *to die and live by a thing* be a Shakespearian idiasm, its signification is as plain as the nose on one's face. It means of course, *to make that thing a matter of life and death*. The profession or calling of a man is that *by which he dies and lives*, i. e. by which he lives, and failing which he dies. In the face of this simple exposition, emendation is a sheer impertinence.

3. Not unfrequently we meet, in the pages of Shakespeare, with a word or phrase which, though sounding strange to us, was familiar enough in his day, and may perhaps still retain a technical use. Here are two examples in point. In 2 Hen. IV., iv. 1, we find Westmoreland thus sharply interrogating Archbishop Scroop,

> Wherefore doe you so ill translate your selfe,
> Out of the Speech of Peace, that beares such grace,
> Into the harsh and boystrous Tongue of Warre?
> Turning your Bookes to Graves, your Inke to Blood,
> Your Pennes to Launces, and your Tongue divine
> To a lowd Trumpet, and a Point of Warre.—Folio 1623.

For *Graves* Warburton would read *glaives*, and Steevens, *greaves*, and it is not easy to decide between them. But what can justify any tampering with the concluding expression, *a point of war?* What can excuse such a conjecture as *report of war*, which stands in manuscript in the Perkins Folio, and in Mr Collier's one-volume edition, or Mr Singer's miserable gloss, *a bruit of war?* Ignorance only; yet such ignorance is hardly credible; for not only was the expression *a point of war* as common as blackberries in Shakespeare's day, *but is still in technical use.* It now means a drum-call, such as the ruffle-beat on parade, when the colours are unfurled. Steele in *The Tatler* used it in the same sense. It occurs frequently in Scott's novels (e. g. *Waverley*, 1st ed., ii. 4 ; *Woodstock*, 1826, i. 21 & 142 ;

and *The Bride of Lammermoor*, 1819, 247), where it always means a trumpet-call. It is also of very common occurrence in the old dramatists (See Staunton's illustrated edition of *Shakespeare*, i. 603.)

Our other example is from *Coriolanus*, v. 5, where Aufidius says of Coriolanus,

> [I] holpe to reape the Fame
> Which he did end all his; and tooke some pride
> **To do my selfe this wrong** (Folio 1623.)

There is not the faintest obscurity about this metaphor; and nothing in the passage but the inflection ' holpe ' is entirely obsolete, and that of course never stuck with anybody.* The whole force of suspicion has fallen on the unoffending verb, *end!* Why, in the name of common sense? Aufidius says that he helped Coriolanus to reap the crop, but that Coriolanus *ended* it, and made it his own. Certainly no difficulty in this phraseology would be presented to the mind of the rudest midland farm-labourer. We may still hear the farmers of Worcestershire and Herefordshire employ that verb in a technical sense in speaking of their crops.

Milton applies it to thrashing out the corn, but not, we think, in a technical sense

---

* Dr Alexander Schmidt explains the passage thus. " I helped to gather the harvest which he consummated as his alone. Perhaps [*end* is] a technical phrase of harvest-work." (*Shakespeare-Lexicon*, 1874.) It certainly is so. But to *reap* is not to *gather*. *Ending* a crop is *gathering* it. A well-ended crop is one that is secured in good condition, or has " made a good end."

5

When in one night ere glimpse of morn
His shadowy flail hath thresh'd the corn,
That ten day-labourers could not *end.*

These points were very justly taken by Mr W. R. Arrowsmith in a sensible, but exceedingly scurrilous and ill-written pamphlet entitled, *The Editor of Notes and Queries and his Friend Mr Singer.* (The title makes us wonder why some of the shortest publications have the longest names. One of the Rev. Joseph Hunter's, consisting of barely 23 pages, has a title comprising 68 words and 12 ciphers!) At p. 9, Mr Arrowsmith gives two newspaper-advertisements in which occur the phrases, 'three excellent well-ended wheatricks,' and 'a rick of well-ended hay.' We are almost ashamed of insisting on anything so obvious : but where the suspected phrase 'walks with his head in a crowd of poisonous flies,' it is the duty of the critic at once to come to its aid ; and the more innocent the phrase, the greater is that duty. In this case no less than five substitutes have been proposed for *end* or for *did end,* and three of these have been admitted into the text ! Of these, the one which has found greatest favour is *ear* for *end,* which was proposed by Mr Collier, and, with the transposition of *reap* and *ear,* was adopted by Mr Singer. *To ear* is to plough, or till! : so that Mr Collier's reading makes Aufidius say that he had his share of the harvest which Coriolanus had tilled for himself ; (and even this sense is defective, since 'did ear' belongs to a later time than 'holpe;') but this is just the reversal of what Aufidius meant : for the gist of his complaint was that he had shared the toil with Coriolamus, and not the harvest. So the late Mr W. N. Lettsom came to the rescue, and proposed (*Notes and Queries*, 1st S. vii. 378) the transposition of *ear* and *reap*. But matters were made no better by this : for Fame, as Mr R. W. Arrowsmith promptly pointed out, is the crop ; and though we *reap the crop*, we *ear* not the crop, but the land. It is noticeable that the clever and shrewd, but waspish critic of *Blackwood's Magazine* (Aug., Sept., and Oct. 1853), the merciless castigator of *Gnats and Queries* (as he designated Mr W. J. Thoms' periodical), proposed the same transposition : so wonderfully do wits jump! What a satire on conjectural criticism is this little farce!

4. But what shall we say when a passage is entirely altered on the supposition that a word meant something which it never did mean, and does not mean at present? Yet this has happened to a passage in *Troilus and Cressida*, v. 2. When Troilus finds that Cressid has forsaken him for Diomed, he bursts into a passion of love and indignation, which is in Shakespeare's finest manner. He cries,

> This is, and is not *Cressid* :
> Within my soule there doth conduce a fight
> Of this strange nature, that a thing inseparate
> Divides more wider then the skie and earth :
> And yet the spacious bredth of this division
> Admits no Orifex for a point as subtle
> As *Ariachne's* broken woofe to enter : (Fo. 1623)

Shakespeare elsewhere employs very similar imagery: ' but I am not to say, it is the sea, for it is now the sky: betwixt the firmament and it you cannot thrust a bodkin's point,' *A Winter's Tale*, iii. 3 ; that is, though the sky and the sea are so widely divided, or separated, yet the sea mounts to such a height, that at times a point cannot be inserted between them. To this kind of equivocal division Troilus compares the separation between his heart and Cressid's. In reality the only question that can be rationally raised concerning this speech of Troilus', is as to the name Ariachne. That is the word of the Folio 1623. The quarto of 1609 has Ariachna, and the undated quarto has Ariathna. This variation is thought to favour the view, that the poet confounded the two names, Arachne and Ariadne, and possibly also the web of the former with the clew of the latter. Arachne was the spinner and weaver, and so subtle, i. e. fine-spun (subtilis), was her woof, that when it was woven into the web, Minerva could not see how the web was made, and in a fit of jealousy and revenge tore it to pieces. If Shakespeare did confound the two fables, it was no more than his contemporaries did. Steevens quotes an example from Day's comedy of *Humour out of Breath*, 1608 (Steevens says 1607) :

> in robes
> Richer than that which Ariadne wrought.

Accordingly, we may see, if we like, Ariadne in both Ariathna and Ariachne : * but after all it may

* Milton made as great a mistake when he attributed to the eglan-

have been a custom of the time to write Ariachne for
Arachne, if the metre required the additional syllable;
and we know that poets and dramatists enjoyed a very
wide discretion in the presentation of proper names.

The point is of no moment. What it is of moment for us to see is that by Ariachne Shakespeare
meant the spider into which Arachne was transformed,
and which in Greek bears the same name; and that the
woof he meant was finer than was ever produced by human
hand, viz. the woof of the spider's web—those delicate
transverse filaments which cross the main radial threads
or *warps,* and which are perhaps the nearest material
approach to mathematical lines! Thus has Shakespeare
in one beautiful allusion wrapt up in two or three little
words the whole story of Arachne's metamorphosis, the
physical fact of the fineness of the woof-filaments of a
spider's web, and an antithesis, effective in the highest
degree, to the vastness of the yawning space between
earth and heaven! For what orifice could be imagined
more exquisitely minute than the needle's eye which

tine the properties of the clematis. In *The Flower of Friendshippe,*
Glomond Tylney, 1568 [8vo], we have, 'All the whole arbour above
over our heades, &c., was * * * wreathed above with the
sweete bryer or eglantine,' &c. In the *Faery Queen,* b. xi. c. 5, st
29, Spenser describes an arbour,

> 'Through which the fragrant eglantine did spred
> His prickling armes, entrayled with roses red.'

Yet Milton speaks of

> 'Thro' the sweet briar or the vine,
> Or the *twisted* eglantine';

would not admit the spider's woof to thread it? And all this argosy has been wrecked by two transpositions.

The late Mr Thomas Keightley, a gentleman held in honour for his school histories, rather than for his unfortunate criticisms on Shakespeare, proposed in *Notes and Queries* (2nd S. ix. 358) what he considered an emendation of the passage we are considering; and subsequently had the temerity to incorporate this change with the text of a complete edition of Shakespeare's works. Observing that his great precursor Beckett had proposed to read,

> Subtile as Arachne's unbroken woof
> Admits no orifex for a point to enter,

whereby that monster had demonstrated to the world that he did not know the meaning of *woof*, Mr Keightley undertook to amend the one line before adopting the other. The great gain, in his view, was that Ariachne had her eye put out, while the 'spacious breadth' was compared to Ariachne's *web!* So he read,

> And yet the spacious breadth of this division,
> As subtle as Arachne's broken woof,
> Admits no orifex for a point to enter.

Unfortunately, this is rank nonsense. How can a 'spacious breadth' be as subtle, or fine-spun, as a thread? Of course, it is easy to see that the whole farrago sprung from the one wretched blunder of taking a *woof* (which ever did and still does mean a thwart or cross-thread) to mean a *web*.

Again, we feel almost ashamed to have to resort to

minute explanation of what every educated Englishman ought to know. In the operation of weaving, the threads which are stretched on the loom are called the *warp*, or *warps*, and the single thread which is carried through them by means of the shuttle is called the *woof*; and the two combined in a texture are called the *web*. This three-fold distinction has been scrupulously observed by all accurate writers from very early times. One or two examples of the use of *woof*, from the literature of Shakespeare's day, may be acceptable, though supererogatory.

' *S. Hierome* would have *Paula* to handle woll, * * and learne to dress it, and to holde and occupie a rocke, [distaff] with a wooll basket in her lap, and turne the spindle, and drawe forth the thread with her own fingers. And *Demetrias* * * he bad have wooll in her hands, and her selfe either to spinne, to warpe, or else winde spindles in a case for to throw *woofe* off, and to winde on clews the spinnings of others, and to order such as should be woven. * * * For should I call him a weaver that never learned to weave, nor to draw the *woffe*, nor to cast the shuttle, nor strike the web with the slaye.' Richard Hyrde's translation of L. Vives' *Instruction of a Christian Woman*, Book i. chap. 3, and Book ii. chap. 4.

5. In not a few cases the idiom of Shakespeare's day has been overlooked by every editor, and in some passages in his text the construction has been altered to

make the unrecognised idiom square with modern usage
The most flagrant case that occurs to us, is that of 'the
suppression of the relative as subject', which, in a particular connection, has always created difficulty with the
editors.   Where the relative is suppressed before an
auxiliary verb, the sense has always been too obvious to
be overlooked   besides, in the case of its suppression
before some tense of the verb *to be*, the practice still pre-
vails in verse, and in epistolary prose.   In the *Tempest*,
v 1, Prospero says to Alonzo and Sebastian,

> A solemne Ayre, and the best comforter,
> To an unsettled fancie, Cure thy braines
> (Now uselesse) boile within thy skull : there stand
> For you are Spell-stopt.   (Folio 1623)

Now in the first place, as two persons are addressed,
and 'you' is the pronoun properly applied to them in
the fourth line, it can hardly be doubted that the possessive pronoun 'thy' in the second and third lines is
an error for *the*.   Persons who have collated the old
copies are familiar with this and similar misprints ; the
pronouns being under a singular fatality.   Making this
simple and necessary correction, and adopting modern
spelling and punctuation, the passage will stand thus

> A solemn air, and the best comforter
> To an unsettled fancy, cure the brains
> (Now useless) boil within the skull : &c.

To modern ears this construction sounds awkward :
accordingly Pope, having no sense of humour, altered
'boile' into *boil'd*.   It was a phrase of the time to say,

that a man's brains boil or are boiling, when he is mad or doting. In Chettle's play of *Hoffman*, in the last scene, the hero, who, strange to relate, manages to converse with his tormentors after he is crowned with the traitor's red-hot iron crown, says,

> Ay, so;—boil on, thou foolish, idle brain,
> For giving entertainment to love's thoughts!

'Boiled brains' is in Shakespeare (*A Winter's Tale,* iii. 3), but the phrase is humorous; and otherwise inapplicable to the men whom Prospero's spell had made frantic: whose brains were *boiling*, not *boiled*. The editors, having as little sense of humour as Pope, have all adopted his abominable gloss. The Rev. Wm. Harness, however, not long before his death privately imparted to us his reading of the passage, which was on this wise: a note of admiration being placed after fancy', continue thus:

> Sure thy brains
> (Now useless) boil within thy skull: &c.

which then seemed to us, and still seems, as imbecile as it is unnecessary. It is as plain as the nose on one's face that the above is an instance of 'the suppression of the relative as subject' before the verb 'boil'. Paraphrase the passage thus: 'Let a solemn air—which is the best comforter to an unsettled fancy—cure the brains [which], now useless, boil within the skull.' 'An unsettled fancy' is a deranged mind, or 'uncertain thought' (as in *Measure for Measure*), 'settled' being Shakespeare's ordinary word for expressing soundness of mind;

and 'fancy' or phantasy, being equivalent to the faculty
we call imagination.

With this example of the idiom in question compare
the following :

> He loved me well * delivered it to me.—
> > *Two Gentlemen of Verona*, iv. 4.

> I have a mind * presages me such thrift.—
> > *Merchant of Venice*, i. 1.

> > But let your reason serve
> To make the truth appear, where it seems hid,
> And hide the false * seems true.—*Measure for Measure*, v. 1.

> Besides our nearness to the king in love
> Is near the hate of those * love not the king.—*Rich. II.*, ii. 2.

> > What wreck discern you in me
> * Deserves your pity ?—*Cymbeline*, i. 7.

> > Why am I bound
> By any generous bond to follow him
> *Follows his Taylor, haply so long untill
> The follow'd make pursuit ?—*The Two Noble Kinsmen*, i. 2.

> > > Only you,
> Of all the rest, are he * commands his love.—*Volpone*, i. 1.

> O then I find that I am bound,
> Upon a wheel * goes ever round.—
> > *Ariosto's Seven Planets*, &c. 1611.
> > The Second Elegy (Appendix), p. 15.

The asterisk in each example shows where the relative
(be it *which* or *who*) is to be understood.

6. Sometimes a word or idiotism presents no kind
of difficulty, yet the passage is meaningless to modern
readers, owing to the loss of some allusion of the time,
which every one then understood in a moment.   For

example: in *Love's Labours Lost*, v. 1, Armado says to Holofernes, 'I do beseech thee, remember thy courtesy, I beseech thee, apparel thy head.' Neither Capell nor Malone understood it, and they therefore proposed emendations. The latter wished to insert *not* 'remember not thy courtesy', i. e. pay no further regard to courtesy, but replace thy hat: as we should now say, 'do not stand on ceremony with me.' This was an absurd proposal, seeing that the phrase is frequent with the early dramatists; and in a curtailed form occurs in *Hamlet.* Yet Mr Dyce (*Few Notes*, p. 56) adopted Malone's conjecture. But he returned to the old text at the instance of the writer, who gave in the *Illustrated London News* a complete defense of the old reading, from a manuscript note of Mr Staunton's which will now be found in his edition of *Shakespeare*, vol. i. p. 83. Mr Dyce on this occasion did not remember his courtesy: not only did he fail to acknowledge this service and assign to Mr Staunton the credit of the restoration, but wrote contemptuously of the notes, of which this was one, evidently not perceiving that one and all were Mr Staunton's. (See Dyce's *Shakespeare*, 1853. Vol. i. p. ccxvi., and p. 581, note (13).)

But the origin of the expression, 'remember thy courtesy', has never been given. It arose, we think, as follows: the courtesy was the temporary removal of the hat from the head, and that was finished as soon as the hat was replaced. If any one from ill-breeding or over-politeness stood uncovered for a longer time than was necessary to perform the simple act of courtesy, the person so saluted reminded him of the fact, that the removal of the hat was a courtesy : and this was expressed by the euphemism, ' Remember thy courtesy ', which thus implied, ' Complete your courtesy, and replace your hat.'

Here is another example in point. In the *Merry Wires of Windsor*, ii. 3, the host says to Dr Caius, ' I will bring thee where Mistress Anne is, at a farm-house a-feasting, and thou shalt woo her. Cried game ? said I well ? '

' Cried game ' has been superseded in several modern editions by ' Cried I aim ', a conjecture of Douce's. Various other substitutes have been proposed. But why should the old text be superseded ? There can hardly be a doubt that under the words ' Cried game ', if authentic, there lurks an allusion of the time which has now to be hunted out. If ' cried game ? ' be either *Is it cried game ?* or *Cried I game ?* we apprehend the allusion is not far to seek. In hare-hunting, a person was employed and paid to find the hare ' muzing on her meaze ', or, as we say, in her form. He was called the hare-finder. When he had found her, he first cried Soho ! to betray the fact to the pursuers ; he then proceeded to put her up, and ' give her courser's law '. What, then, can ' Cried I game ? ' mean but *Did I cry game ? Did I cry Soho ?* In the play before us, the pursuit was after Mistress Anne Page. She was the hare, and the host undertook to betray her whereabouts to Dr Caius, in order that he might urge his love-suit.

7. Some expressions in the text, which were then, and still are, grammatical and significant, have been altered, because their force is spent. They once had a sort of proverbial point, which is now wholly gone from them; hence they readily fall a prey to ingenious guessers. One instance will be sufficient to exemplify the class. In *As You Like It*, iii. 5, we read,

> Who might be your mother,
> That you insult, exult, and all at once,
> Over the wretched?

If emendation were wanted here, surely a *happier* suggestion was never made than that of Warburton, who proposed to read, *rail* for 'all' Earlier in the same play we have (i. 1),

> 'Thou hast rail'd on thyself.'

Compare also *Lear*, ii. 3,

> being down, insulted, rail'd
> And put upon, &c.

Yet the text is most certainly right. There is hardly a commoner phrase, more especially at the end of a verse, than *and all at once*. Compare *Hen. V.*, i. 1,

> Nor never Hydra-headed wilfulness
> So soon did lose his seat, and all at once,
> As in this King.

The reader who desires to see other corroborative instances from writers of the time may consult Mr Staunton's illustrated edition of *Shakespeare*, vol. ii. p. 65. In this case the Cambridge Editors give us a truly wonderful collection of conjectures, one of which is Warburton's *domineer!* and this feat of dulness is capped by another, which consists of four French words!

8. But more curious still, there are passages which have occasioned a considerable amount of discussion, and have even received emendation, not on account of anything difficult or corrupt in the construction, but simply because no one among the swarm of critics had seized the central or leading notion of the speaker. The two following from the same play, which are selected from many cases in point, may serve as samples of the class. These are also in *As You Like It.* In iii. 2, Rosalind plies Celia with some questions respecting Orlando: and having reminded her friend, that though she (Rosalind) is caparisoned like a man, she has a woman's curiosity, adds,

> ' One inch of delay more, is a South-sea of discoverie. I pre'thee tell me who it is quickly, and speak apace: I would thou couldst stammer, &c. Is he of God's making? What manner of man? Is his head worth a hat? or his chin worth a beard?'

Reading this passage in the folio, we have sought in vain for some explanation of the fact that its central or leading notion has always been missed. Here we have a tale of questions— *coup sur coup*—falling as thick as hail upon the devoted Celia. See how many things she is called upon to *discover;* and then say whether she has not incurred a laborious and vexatious duty by her *delay* in answering the first question. How plain it is that her *inch* of delay has cast upon her a *South Sea* —a vast and unexplored ocean—of discovery. The more Celia delays her revelation as to who the man is, the more she will have to reveal about him. Why? Because Rosalind fills up the delay (increases it, in fact,) with fresh interrogatories, whereby Celia becomes lost in a South Sea of questions.

There is surely some fatality about this play, for we observe several other passages in it, which, without more than the shadow of a pretence, have been altered in every, or almost every, edition. For instance, in ii. 6, Jaques says :

> Hee, that a Foole doth very wisely hit,
> Doth very foolishly, although he smart
> Seeme senselesse of the bob. If not,
> The Wise-man's folly is anathomiz'd
> Even by the squandering glances of the foole.
>
> Folio 1623.

Theobald, being conscious of a hitch in the sense, proposed 'Not to seem senselesse' for 'Seeme senselesse'. In this lead he has been usually followed, even by the Cambridge Editors. Had they seized the central notion of the passage, they would not have done so. Why does a fool do *wisely* in hitting a wise man? Because, through the vantage of his folly, he puts the wise man 'in a strait betwixt two', to put up with the smart of the bob, without dissembling, and so incur the consequential awkwardness of having to do so—which makes him feel foolish enough—or, to put up with the smart, *and dissemble it*, which entails the secondary awkwardness of the dissimulation—which makes him

feel still more foolish. Taking the former alternative,
i. e. 'If not' ('If *he do* not') his 'folly is anatomized
even by the squandring glances of the fool'; taking the
latter alternative, he makes a fool of himself in the eyes
of almost everybody else. So the fool gets the advantage both ways. There is a passage in a paper of De
Quincey's called 'Literary Novitiate,' published in vol.
i. of *Literary Reminiscences* (Ticknor and Field's
edition), which has a special bearing on the above
passage. At page 25 we read, 'Awkwardness at
the least—and too probably, as a consequence of
that, affectation and conceit—follow hard upon the consciousness of special notice or admiration. The very
attempt to disguise embarrassment too often issues in a
secondary and more marked embarrassment.' How
plain, then, is the sense of the passage we are considering. Jaques asks for 'the motley', in order that he
may have a fool's privilege of making a fool of every
wise man. In *Othello*, i. 3, is a passage which may
serve to illustrate this.

> What cannot be preserved when fortune takes,
> Patience her injury a mockery makes.
> The robb'd that smiles, steals something from the thief;
> He robs himself, that spends a bootless grief.

Observing that the line,

> Seeme senselesse of the bob.   If not.

is too short, we think it probable that the words *he do*
originally formed part of it. Be that as it may, 'If not'
must mean 'If he do not'. 'Very foolishly' should be

placed in crotchets : perhaps 'very wisely' should be so also.

9. A strictly methodical discussion of classes of readings, even if it were practicable, would not present any very great advantage : so we have not attempted it. We will now proceed to consider two of the cases in which Shakespeare has metaphorically employed the image of *a sea :* viz. 'a sea of wax,' and 'a sea of troubles.'

The pedantic poet in *Timon of Athens*, i. 1, addresses the painter in the following tumid and bombastic terms

> You see this confluence, this great flood of visitors.
> I have in this rough work shaped out a man [*shewing his manuscript*]
> Whom this beneath world both embrace and hug
> With amplest entertainment : my free drift
> Halts not particularly, but moves itself
> In a wide sea of wax : no levell'd malice
> Infects one comma of the course I hold
> But flies an eagle's flight, bold and forth on,
> Leaving no tract behind

In this passage, 'my free drift' and 'a wide sea of wax' are contrasted with the notion of 'halting particularly' and 'levell'd malice'. In other words, the poet is contrasting generality with particularity. The visitors who throng the presence-chamber of Lord Timon are compared by the poet to a sea, or arm of the sea, when the tide is rising, and are therefore designated a 'confluence' and a 'great flood'. Timon is said to be embraced 'with amplest entertainment' by this flood ; and the poet disclaiming particular per-

sonal censure, asserts, in a metaphor probably derived
from Archery, that 'no levell'd malice infects one
comma', i e. not a single clause, in his poem. It is
the antecedent sentence which contains the stumbling-
block.   What is the meaning of 'a wide sea of wax'?
Every one knows that the verb *to wax* means, to grow;
and the old English writers employ it indifferently of
increase or decrease; a thing, with them, may wax
greater or smaller, stronger or weaker. *To wax* was to
change condition simply.   But more strictly it was and
is still used in opposition to *wane*. If anything changes
its condition, it either waxes or wanes.   In this restricted sense Shakespeare in several places uses the
verb *to wax*, of the sea.

> Who marks the waxing sea grow wave by wave.—
> *Titus Andronicus*, iii. 1.

> His pupil age
> Man-enter'd thus, he waxed like a sea.—*Coriolanus*, ii. 1.

The older editors and commentators seem not to
have had the faintest suspicion of the meaning of the
expression, 'a wide sea of wax'.   Hanmer and Steevens
explain it as an allusion to the Roman and early English practice of writing with a style on tablets coated
with wax, so that the poet in *Timon* must be supposed
literally to have 'shaped out' his man in wax, almost as
much so as if he had modelled him.   All the editors
have followed this lead.   Mr Dyce to the last was con-
firmed in this interpretation; but Mr Staunton, who
had once accepted it, was at length conducted to the

extraordinary conclusion, that 'wax' was a press-error
for *tar!* Besides this, the only emendation attempted
is Mr Collier's *verse*. Very strange indeed is all this
speculation, in the face of the certain fact, that the substantive, *wax*, occurs elsewhere in Shakespeare in an
allied sense.

Chief Justice. What! you are as a candle, the better part burnt out.
Falstaff. A wassail candle, my lord; all tallow: if I did say of wax,
my growth would approve the truth —2 *Hen. IV.*, i. 2

It is all very well to say that this is a quibble or
pun: it is so: but such a pun would be insufferable—
not to say impossible—unless there were a substantive
wax, meaning growth, on which to make the pun. It
is, indeed, open to question whether *wax* be used in this
sense, in the proverbial phrase 'a man of wax', which
occurs in *Romeo and Juliet*, i. 3.* 'A wide sea of wax'

* I formerly accepted Mr Brae's view, that in Ben Jonson's post-
humous fragment *The Fall of Mortimer*, the word *waxe* had the
sense of personal aggrandisement: but I am now convinced that Mr
Dyce was quite right in referring the word in question to the waxen
seal attached to the Earl's patent of nobility. Evidently Mortimer is
noting the *outward* insignia of his rank—viz. his 'crownet', his 'robes',
and the Great Seal, which *he bore in his hand*. This last is a point
overlooked by Mr Dyce. Mr Brae, who has privately retracted his interpretation, refers me to *Nobilitas Politica vel Civilis*, by Robert
Glover, Somerset Herald: edited in 1608 by his nephew Thomas
Milles. He tells us that an Earl 'bore a patent with the Great Seal
pendent by Cord and Tassel.' Mr Brae seems to have been misled by
the two lines which follow 'crownet, robes, and waxe', in Jonson's
play; in which he saw a possible allusion to the poet's speech in *Timon*.

> There is a fate that flies with towering spirits
> Home to the mark, and never checks at Conscience.

But the metaphor is taken from hawking.

seems to be merely an affected and pedantic mode of indicating a sea that widens with the flood.

In *Hamlet*, iii. 1, we read :

> Whether 'tis nobler in the mind to suffer
> The slings and arrows of outrageous fortune,
> Or to take arms against a sea of troubles,
> And by opposing end them:

The question implies an option, either to endure the troubles or to end them ' with a bare bodkin ' or otherwise. If 'a sea of troubles' be taken to mean *a troublous sea* (somewhat as in the passage we have just considered 'a sea of wax' means *a waxing sea,* or a sea at flood tide), the phrase ' to take arms against a sea of troubles' expresses as futile a feat as ' to wound the still-closing waters'. Would Shakespeare have put such a catachresis into the mouth of the philosophical Hamlet ? The doubt thus engendered has manifested itself, as usual, in a plentiful crop of emendations, which in this case are all ingenious, with the exception of one proposed by the late Mr Samuel Bailey. By far the best is Mr A. E. Brae's conjecture of *assay* for 'a sea'. In the presence of that we think it impertinent to name its rivals. It is not only singularly clever, but it gives a sense, force, and dignity to the passage, which, thus emended, is in Shakespeare's best manner. But this is not enough.

In the first place let us clearly realize the fact, that the metaphor, *a sea of troubles, sorrows, griefs, dangers,* &c., is as old as the hills, and is found in all languages :

and it is admirably expressive of the two attributes of those sorrows that come ' in battalions', their multiplicity, and their power to overwhelm. Accordingly no defense or illustration of the figure is needed. Moreover it has been contended by many critics, as Johnson, Malone, Warburton (in his second thoughts), Caldecott, De Quincey, and Mr Staunton, that the want of consistency or integrity in this metaphor is no argument against Shakespeare having written the passage as it stands. Caldecott (*Specimen of a New Edition of Shakespeare*, 1819, p. 65) puts it thus : ' He uses it [the metaphor] himself everywhere and in every form : and the integrity of his metaphor is that which by him is of all things the least thought of.' In support of this assertion Caldecott refers to three passages in Shakespeare, not one of which bears it out. The fact is, that Shakespeare employs *sea* figuratively eight times : viz. *Timon of Athens*, i. 1, 'sea of wax'; and iv. 2, 'sea of air': *Pericles*, v. 1, ' sea of joys': *Hen. VIII.*, iii. 2, 'sea of glory'; and ii. 4, 'sea of conscience': 1 *Hen. VI.*, iv. 7, 'sea of blood' : *Lucrece*, st. 158, 'sea of care'; and the instance in question. In every case, except the last which is on its trial, the integrity of the metaphor is sufficiently preserved. That, however, in *Timon of Atheas*, iv. 2, has been thought questionable ; and Mr Richard Garnett (*Athenæum*, Oct. 15, 1859), after quoting the lines,

> Leak'd is our bark,
> And we, poor mates, stand on the dying-deck,
> Hearing the surges threat : we must all part
> Into *this sea of air*,

remarks—' I, for one, can neither understand the phrase in italics, nor correct it.' Without asserting that these lines were written by Shakespeare, we may very readily illustrate their meaning. ' Part ', of course, is *depart;* * and the ' sea of air ' is that into which the soul, freighting his wrecked bark, the body, must at length take its flight. Compare with the above, the following from Drayton's *Battle of Agincourt :*

> Now where both armies got upon that ground,
> As on a stage, where they their strengths must try,
> Whence *from the width of many a gaping wound*
> There's *many a soul into the air must fly.*

As to Shakespeare's metaphor in the passage under consideration, ' a sea of troubles ', it occurs once in the *Faerie Queen* (Book VI. c. ix. st. 31); and the sea is otherwise employed metaphorically by Spenser in many places (see the *Faerie Queen*, Book I. c. xii. st. 14 : Book III. c. iv. st. 8, &c.), but not once does he do violence to the metaphor. It is also frequently found in prose works of the time. In Richard Morysine's translation of L. Vives' *Introduction to Wysedom*, Book IV., we have ' sea of evils '; and in Andrew Kingsmyll's *Comforts in Afflictions* (fol. 6) we have ' seas of sorrows ' : and in both cases is the integrity of the metaphor preserved. Are we, then, to believe that Shakespeare departed from this conscientious custom in one passage,

---

* The converse is the case with an expression in the Marriage Service; so in *Green's Groatsworth of Wit* ' but I am yours till death us depart.'

where *a sea* is not an improbable misprint for *assay?*

We are thus presented with the horns of a dilemma : viz. on the one hand the imputation of a lame metaphor to Shakespeare's most philosophic character, and on the other, a conjectural emendation. Now it seems to us that there is a way out of this dilemma—a middle course which has hitherto escaped the notice of the critics. One consideration of the highest importance has been entirely ignored. When Hamlet talked of ending his sea of troubles, or, as he afterwards describes it, shuffling off his mortal coil,* he had a covert consciousness, a *conscience* in fact, which stayed the hand he would have raised against his own life ; viz. that this so-called ending and shuffling off, was a mere delusion, just as much so as repelling the advancing waves of the sea with shield and spear. Is not the metaphor, then, sound and whole? If there be an incongruity in the notion of taking arms, offensively or defensively, against the sea, is there not just as great an incongruity in using 'a bare bodkin' against the soul—the immortal part, which (as Raleigh has it) 'no stab can kill'? But, in fact, that seeming incongruity is defensible, quite apart from the metaphor. The late Mr Samuel Bailey in his discussion of the passage in question has the following re-

---

* Shakespeare represents the human body under various figures : a *coil* : a *case* : a *frame* : a *machine* : a *vesture* : a *heft* : a *motion* or puppet : &c. It has been contended that in Hamlet's speech, the 'mortal coil' is the coil, i.e. trouble or turmoil, incident to man's mortal state : but the analogies are too strong in favour of the 'mortal coil' being what Fletcher calls the 'case of flesh' (*Bonduca.* iv. 1).

mark : 'The objection is not to the metaphorical de-
signation *a sea of troubles,* [—who ever said it was?]
but to the figurative absurdity implied in "taking up
arms against a sea of troubles", or indeed against any
other sea, literal or imaginary. I question whether any
instance is to be found of such a fight in the whole
compass of English Literature'. (*The Received Text of
Shakespeare,* p. 39.) Why restrict the search to English
Literature? But the instance is to be found in various
literatures. In Ritson's *Memoirs of the Celts* (p. 118)
occurs the following passage, which is a translation of
one in Ælian:

> ' Of all men I hear that the Celts are most ready to
> undergo dangers. ❋ ❋ ❋ So base, indeed, do
> they consider it to fly, that frequently they will not
> escape out of houses tumbling down and falling in
> upon them, nor even out of those burning, though
> themselves are ready to be caught by the fire.
> Many, also, oppose the overwhelming sea : there
> are some, likewise, who taking arms rush upon the
> waves, and sustain their attack, extending their
> naked swords and spears, in like manner as if they
> were able to terrify or wound them.'

The same tradition is referred to by Aristotle in his
Eudemian Ethics, iii. 1 :

> οἷον οἱ Κελτοὶ πρὸς τὰ κύματα ὅπλα ἀπαντῶσι
> λαβόντες.

See also Arist. Nich. Eth. iii. 7.

We think, then, Hamlet's soliloquy might be fairly paraphrased thus :

> 'To exist: or to cease to exist : that is the question
> for me to decide.   Whether it is the nobler part
> to endure the outrages of fortune, and to dare the
> surrounding sea of troubles ; or to imitate the
> fabled feats of the Celts, and " taking arms rush
> upon the waves."   Doubtless it is the nobler to
> endure unshaken ; and is it not also more pru-
> dent ?   For, it seems probable, that the attempt to
> end our troubles by self-destruction would be as
> futile as that of the Celts to assail the ocean ;
> and that after death itself we should find ourselves
> overwhelmed by evils of which we know nothing,
> and which therefore, for aught we know, may be
> greater than those from which we should have
> escaped.   Thus does conscience make cowards of
> us all.'

All things considered, then, in the case before us, we elect to adhere to the received text, and to refuse to allow even the most admirable of emendations to allure us from our allegiance to that consistent metaphor which has all the external evidences of authenticity.

While on this famous soliloquy, we may as well note that

> The undiscovered country from whose bourn
> No traveller returns

is the allegorical country of the Meropes, well known to every reader in Shakespeare's day. In the fifth discourse of the Spanish Mandevile (London, 1600, p. 126), Bernado, one of the interlocutors, says,

'That which I will tell you is out of Theopompus, alleaged by Ælianus in his book *De varia Historia*. [It is in Æl. Var. Hist. iii. 18.] This Sylenus * * * * in one communication that hee had with King Mydas, discoursed unto him, that out of this Land or world in which wee live * * * * there is another Land so great that it is infinite and without measure * * * * and the men which dwell therein are twise so great as we are, and their life twise as long * * * * . There were in other provinces thereof certain people called Meropes, who inhabited many and great Citties, within the bounds of whose Country there was a place called Anostum, which word signifieth, a place whence there is no returne: this Country, saith he, is not cleare and light, neither yet altogether darke, but between both, through the same runne two Rivers, the one of delight, the other of griefe', &c. *

It is noteworthy, too, that 'the undiscovered

---

* For these two illustrations from Ælian we are indebted to our friend Dr Sebastian Evans: who in the passage from *Hamlet* would omit the pronoun after 'end,' understanding by that verb *die*.

country' is not mentioned in the 4to, 1603. Shakespeare may have read this passage in Ælian between 1602 and 1604, in which latter year the first enlarged *Hamlet* was published, containing the allusion to Anostum.

10. Some of the obscurities in Shakespeare's text arise from the consilience of two sources of perplexity. Here is one example, in which a word employed in an obsolete sense forms part of a phrase which is itself of peculiar construction. In *Hamlet*, i. 4, Horatio tries to dissuade Hamlet from accompanying the ghost, lest it should

> assume some other horrible form,
> Which might deprive your sovereignty of reason,
> And draw you into madness.

The verb *to deprive* is at present used with the same construction as *bereave* or *rob;* but in Shakespeare it corresponds to our *ablate.* Thus in *Lucrece*, st. clxx.:

> 'Tis honour to deprive dishonour'd life.

And again in st. ccli.:

> That life was mine, which thou hast here depriv'd.

But the passage from Hamlet contains yet another source of perplexity, viz. to ' deprive your *sovereignty of reason*', i. e. to deprive the sovereignty of your reason; or, as we should more naturally say, to deprive your reason of its sovereignty*: in view of which the Rev Joseph Hunter (*Few Words*) proposed to transpose 'your' and 'of'. In defense of the original text, take the following from a letter of Sir Thomas Dale, 1616 (the year of Shakespeare's death). He calls Virginia, 'one of the goodliest and richest kingdoms in the world, which being inhabited by the king's subjects, will put such a bit into our ancient enemy's mouth as will curb *his hautiness of monarchy.*'

11. Occasionally it is the figurative language of the text which throws the critic on a false scent, and thus leads him to look for a corruption where there is none. The best example which we can call to mind is a passage in *Much Ado About Nothing*, iv. 1. Leonato, learning that Hero has fainted under the shock of her disgrace, cries,

> Do not live, Hero, do not ope thine eyes:
> For, did I think thou wouldst not quickly die,
> Thought I thy spirits were stronger than thy shames,
> Myself would on the rearward of reproaches
> Strike at thy life.

This is the reading of the quarto, which has the spelling *rereward*. The military metaphor has perplexed the critics. The war is between Hero's spirits

---

* It is purely an accident that the objective of 'deprive' is expressed by two substantives connected by *of*, suggesting to the modern reader the construction here given. A learned friend suggests that in some possible poem, entitled (say) 'The Battle of the High and the Low,' the following might occur :

> To make an application to the Bishop,
> Who might deprive the rector of the parish,
> And turn him out of office.

and her shames or reproaches. The latter have, in the
onset, assailed her, and she lies insensible from their
violence. Then says Leonato, if, owing to the sustain-
ing power of her spirits, her reproaches fail to kill her, I
will come, as a reserve, in their rear, and I will slay her
myself. Not perceiving the integrity of the metaphor;
for which 'rearward' (the opposite of *coyward, cayward,*
or *vanguard*) is absolutely required, Mr A. E. Brae, this
time most infelicitously, proposed to read *reword* for
the reading of the folio, 'reward'. This reading would
invest the passage with downright nonsense; for as it
stands, the very deficiency of the reproaches (which are
enough to prostrate, but not to kill her) is the reason for
Leonato's interference: whereas, Mr Brae's reading
would make him say, that if that deficiency were abated,
if their power were recruited, he would then interpose
to do a work of supererogation. Besides, this reading
seems to distinguish between Hero's *shames* and her *reproaches,* which are evidently one and the same. If,
then, the text were faulty, Mr Brae's reading would be
no cure, but even make matters worse. The objection
to *reward,* taken in the old sense of *regard,* or to *reword,*
on the ground of prosody, would be untenable. *Reward*
and *reword* might be indifferently iambuses or trochees.
Relapse, severe, supreme, and *secure* (Shakespeare), *reflect* (Fletcher), *regret* (Drant), *revere* (May), and *recluse*
(Donne), are all occasionally used as trochees. The real
objection to *reward* is, that the sense of *regard* was
already obsolete when Shakespeare wrote: that to *re-*

word is, that it makes Leonato's declaration inconsistent with itself, violates the integrity of the metaphor, and degrades Hero's reproaches (her shames, in fact,) into verbal accusations: ('upon the repetition of these charges' is Mr Brae's paraphrase); to both alike, that the relative text presents no difficulty to the reader who understands the military figure which it involves, and therefore no footing for the conjectural critic. We have, in fact, the same metaphor in Shakespeare's 90th Sonnet, which has also suffered emendation in Mr F. T. Palgrave's *Gem Edition:*

> Oh! do not, when my heart hath scap'd this sorrow
> *Come in the rearward of a conquer'd woe ,*
> Give not a windy night a rainy morrow,
> To linger out a purpos'd overthrow.
> If thou wilt leave me, do not leave me last
> When other petty griefs have done their spite,
> *But in the onset come;* so shall I taste
> At first the very worst of Fortune's might ; &c.

We will give one more example of the same fatality. Shakespeare's figurative use of the word *stain*, whether substantive or verb, is various. The primary notion is that of giving to something a colour from without ; this may be a stain of foulness or otherwise, and *stain* may thus mean *pollute, pollution ;* or somewhat more generally, *dishonour ;* otherwise, *dye, indue* (verb, in Shakespeare's peculiar sense), and therefore *subdue* (verb),—i. e. to a particular attribute or quality ; and again, *infect, infection,* and finally *compromise.* In another view the substantive *stain* may signify the reverse of *foil,* as in *Venus and Adonis,* st. 1, 'stain to all nymphs,' i. e. casting their

charms into the *shade* by comparison with those of
Venus. The passage we have in view, in making these
remarks, is in *Antony and Cleopatra*, iii. 4. Antony
complains to Octavia that her brother has gone to war
against Pompey without reason, and without his (Antony's) concurrence; that he has given him (Antony)
'narrow measure' in speaking of him. This touches his
honour, and he therefore declares that while his wife
goes, as reconciler, between the two triumvirs, he will
give Cæsar a strong motive for making overtures of
friendship. He says,

> The mean time, lady,
> I'll raise the preparation of a war
> Shall *stain* your brother

The metaphor, which once seized can never occasion
the least perplexity, has misled the critics, who have
accordingly attempted to remedy a seeming imperfection, by treating 'stain' as a misprint. Theobald reads
strain; Boswell proposed *stay*, which Mr J P. Collier
adopted. Rann has '*stain*, for *sustain*. Jackson proposed *stun*; and the Cambridge Editors, worst of all, conjecture *slack!* Certainly, had *strain* been in the old text
we should have been well satisfied with it. But while regarding that as *facile princeps* among the proposed substitutes, we hold it quite inferior to the word of the folio.
Compromise would be a dilution of *stain*, in the sense we
believe Shakespeare to have intended. Antony's prepara-
tion was designed to effect a total change in Cæsar's purposes and plans, in fact to induce and subdue him to the

quality of Antony's mind—possibly even to overshadow Cæsar, and impress him with the weight of Antony's personal character. As it seems to us, we lose a sea of meaning by adopting any of the proposed substitutes. Our bard eschewed, for the most part, weak generalities, and, though his word *stain* have a considerable range of meaning, it is preserved from vagueness by its anchorage in the world of sense.

12. Some passages present a cluster of difficulties—so many, in fact, that it cannot be supposed that mere textual corruption can have originated them all. Two salient examples occur respectively in *Measure for Measure*, iii. 1, and *Cymbeline*, v. 4; both relating to death. The former runs thus:

> I, but to die, and go we know not where,
> To lie in cold obstruction, and to rot,
> This sensible warm motion, to become
> A kneaded clod; And the delighted spirit
> To bath in fierie floods, or to recide
> In thrilling Region of thicke-ribbed Ice,
> To be imprison'd in the viewlesse windes
> And blowne with restlesse violence round about
> The pendant world: or to be worse then worst
> Of those, that lawlesse and incertaine thought,
> Imagine howling, 'tis too horrible.   Folio 1623.

The opening of this passage was specially selected by Mr J. M. D. Meiklejohn, in a paper read to the *College of Preceptors*, as an illustration of his assertion that the practice of calling upon a student to write a paraphrase of poetry is useless and absurd: here he pronounced a paraphrase to be impossible. Now a paraphrase is only impossible through some inherent obscurity in the text to be expounded: and surely the more difficult a passage is, the more useful is the paraphrase. To us it appears plain that the practice of calling for a paraphrase is in the highest degree commendable: for it is the only means by which the teacher can discover how far his pupil understands the passage which forms the subject of his study. Not that a paraphrase can by any means convey the whole sense of the original: no paraphrase was ever intended to do that: but it can convey, by analysis and qualification, the greater part of that sense; and surely 'half a loaf is better than no bread.' We do not 'halt particularly' to expound the meaning of 'cold obstruction' or 'delighted spirit:' we would rather call attention to Shakespeare's use of the abstract substantive, as 'Region' and 'thought.' Dyce's first edition thus remarks upon the former word: 'The folio has "Region": but the plural is positively required here on account of "*floods*" in the preceding, and "*winds*" in the following line.' And for the latter he reads, after all the editors, save those of Oxford and Cambridge, '*thoughts.*' That note, if it mean anything, means that Shakespeare employed *Region* in the concrete, and in the modern and ordinary sense: and we have no doubt that Dyce adopted the plural *thoughts* as the nominative to 'imagine.' On the contrary we contend that 'Region' is used in the abstract, and in the radical sense; and that it means *restricted place*, or *con-*

finement * : also, that 'thought' is used in the abstract,
and that it is the objective governed by 'imagine.'
The adjective 'incertain' is employed in a specialised
sense, like the Latin *incertus : certain*, like *certus*, is used
by Shakespeare as the opposite of crazy or mad : e. g.
in *A Midsummer Night's Dream*, i. 1, Demetrius says,

> Relent, sweet Hermia; And Lysander yield
> Thy *crazed* title to my *certain* right ;

and again in ii. 2,

> That the *rude* sea grew *civil* at her song ;
> And *certain* stars shot *madly* from their spheres, &c.

In fact, *certain* and *incertain* are synonyms for *settled*
and *unsettled*, respectively.   (See 'settled senses,' *Winter's Tale*, v. 3 ; and 'unsettled fancy,' *Tempest*, v. 1.)
Accordingly, as we read the passage, the last three lines
may be paraphrased thus :

> 'Or to be in an infinitely worse case than those
> who body forth—or render objective—their own
> lawless and crazed mind.'

The pendant from *Cymbeline*, v. 4, is as follows :

> Most welcome bondage ! For thou art a way,
> I think, to liberty.   Yet am I better
> Than one that's sick o' the gout, since he had rather
> Groan so in perpetuity, than be cured

---

* So Carlyle appears to have understood it : for in his *Heroes and
Hero-worship*, 1842, Lect. iii. p. 135, he quotes the passage *à propos* of Dante's 'soft etherial soul, looking out so stern, implacable, grim-
trenchant, as from *imprisonment of thick-ribbed ice !*' as expressed in
Giotto's portrait.   He is perhaps also glancing at *L'Inferno*, Canto
xxxiv.

By the sure physician, Death; who is the key
To unbar these locks. My conscience! thou art fettered
More than my shanks and wrists. You good gods give me
The penitent instrument to pick that bolt,
Then free for ever! Is 't enough I'm sorry?
So children temporal fathers do appease;
Gods are more full of mercy. Must I repent?
I cannot do it better than in gyves
Desired more than constrain'd. To satisfy,
(If of my freedom 'tis the main part) take
No stricter render of me than my all
I know you are more clement than viled men,
Who of their broken debtors take a third,
A sixth, a tenth, letting them thrive again
On their abatement; **that 's not my desire:**
For Imogen's dear life **take mine; and** though
'Tis not so dear, yet **'tis a life: you coin'd it.**
'Tween man and man they weigh not every stamp;
Though light, take pieces for the figure's sake;
You rather, mine being yours and so, Great Powers,
If you will take this audit, take this **life,**
And cancel these cold bonds.

Of the passage from 'Must I repent,' down to 'my
all,' Mr Staunton writes, 'It is, we fear, hopelessly
incurable.' To which we can only answer, that we
see there no corruption whatever! Difficulty there is,
but none that does not disappear by the simple process of
elucidation. In our judgment the entire passage is one of
those in which the bard displays at once his wealth of
knowledge and his fertility and felicity of language. Its
terseness, along with a technical and figurative use of
words, has misled all the critics : and, as the result of
their industry, we have only systematic misprision and
wanton innovation. In Shakespeare-criticism we learn

to be grateful for negative virtues : and we are really thankful to Mr Staunton for printing the passage intact and entire, and sparing us the pain of conjectural corruption. Posthumus rejoices in his bodily thraldom, because its issue will be death, which will set him free : certainly from bodily bondage, and possibly from spiritual bondage—the worse of the twain. So he prays for 'the penitent instrument to pick *that* bolt,' the bolt which fetters his conscience worse than the cold gyves constrain his shanks and wrists : that is, for the means of a repentance which may be efficacious for pardon and absolution. He then enters into these means in detail, following the order of the old Churchmen : viz. sorrow for sin, or *attrition* : 'Is't enough I am sorry ?' &c. : then penance, which was held to convert attrition into *contrition* : 'Must I repent ?' &c. : then *satisfaction* for the wrong done. As to this last he says, if the main condition of his spiritual freedom be that, ('To satisfy,') let not the gods *with that object* take a stricter render than his all—his life. These are the three parts of absolution. The third he expands in the last clause. He owns that his debt exceeds his all. He says, in effect,

'Do not call me to a stricter account than the forfeiture of my all *towards* payment. Take my all, and give me a receipt, not on account, but in full of all demands. Earthly creditors take of their debtors a fraction of their debt and less than their all, 'letting them thrive again on their abatement' :

but I do not desire that indulgence of your cle-
mency. Take life for life—my all : and though it
is not worth so much as Imogen's, yet 'tis a life,
and of the same divine origin : a coin from the
same mint. Between man and man light pieces
are current for the sake of the figure stamped upon
them : so much the rather should the gods take
my life, which is in their own image, though it is
not so dear or precious as Imogen's *.'

The old writers compared the hindrances of the body
to gyves : so Walkington in *The Optick Glasse of Hum-
ors*, 1607, folio 11, 'Our bodies were the prisons and
bridewils of our soules, wherein they lay manicled and
fettered in Gives', &c.† : and when Posthumus says
'Cancel these cold bonds,' he means free the soul from
the body : but the epithet 'cold' has reference to the
material gyves, which were of iron : cf. *The Two Noble
Kinsmen*, iii. 1, where Palamon says, 'Quit me of these
cold gyves '—i. e. knock off my fetters.

Such passages as these two serve as admirable illus-
trations of the novel position taken by a writer in the
Times of Sept. 29, 1863, in a review of *The Cambridge
Edition of Shakespeare:* 'There never was an author
who less required note or comment than Shakespeare.'
It is quite true that the mass of readers are content to

* For the keys to these two passages I am indebted to Mr Hugh
Carleton of Auckland, N. Z., and to the late Rev. W. W. Berry, Pre-
bendary of S. Paul's.

† He is possibly thinking of the *Phaedo*, 72 and 73

take the text as they find it, and take in as much of **it** as they can without trouble; and that the mass of critics and editors are impatient of the restraint which a thorough and painstaking study of the **text would** impose upon their conjectural fertility—it is so much easier to 'regulate' the text, or to shun the dark places in it, than to elucidate it. MEANWHILE THE STILL LION IS PATIENT AND LONGSUFFERING, AND 'REQUIRES' NEITHER NOTE NOR COMMENT: BUT IS READY TO AVENGE HIMSELF ON SCIOLISTS AND MEDDLERS.

We now hold our hand: but passages upon passages crowd upon us, clamouring for advocacy and defence, which as yet are suffering the crying wrongs of emendation, as if the Promethean bard were here chained to the rock of pedantry, and a critical vulture were preying on his vitals. But we trust we have done enough, both by way of warning and of criticism, to show that ignorance of the spelling, language, and customs of Shakespeare's day, is an absolute disqualification for the serious work of criticism, even more so than the insensibility of such men as Steevens and Johnson.

The text is beset with difficulties to the ordinary reader, which are occasioned far more by the presence of obsolete phraseology and of allusions to obsolete customs and forgotten events than by the accidents of the press; so that to an ignorant reader who is impatient of obscurity profuse emendation is a positive necessity. But unhappily, ignorance, insensibility, and literary ambition concur to convert a reader into a criticaster of Shakespeare's text. The result is, that passages, eminent for their sense and beauty, for the purity of their construction, the selectness of their words, the dignity or fitness of their thoughts, are defaced and marred by the meddling, clumsy boor whose vanity has induced him to play the critic. Such is the fate that has befallen, among many other passages of faultless excellence, that, perhaps the most lovely of all that ever flowed from the great soul of the poet, in which Pericles calls on Helicanus to wound him, lest he should be drowned with the sweetness of 'the great sea of joys' that rushed upon him*: till at length we are glad to find a fitting vent for our grief and indignation in the words of Milton,

> See with what haste these dogs of Hell advance
> To waste and havoc yonder world, which THOU
> Hast made so fair!

---

* We had in mind the late Mr Samuel Bailey's proposal to alter 'sweetness' into *surges*, for publishing which, in our judgment he deserved to stand in the pillory, or do penance in a white sheet, or go woolward and lie in the woollen till he came to a better frame of mind. When we saw his work *On the Received Text of Shakespeare* we thought we had seen the worst possible of Shakespeare-criticism We found ourselves in error there, however, as soon as we saw the now late Mr Thomas Keightley's *Shakespeare Expositor.* In defence of Shakespeare's expression, 'To drown me with their sweetness', if, forsooth, defense were needed, or let us say for its illustration, we might cite the following from Stephen Gosson's *Plays Confuted in Five Actions,* (n d.) sig. B. 4, 'because we are . . . drunken with the sweetness of these vanities.'

CHAPTER V.

ON THE CONJECTURAL EMENDATION OF SHAKESPEARE'S TEXT.

HAPPY indeed shall we be if our remarks induce the verbal critic to *spare* the works of Shakespeare as he *loves* them. But, at the same time, we concede the fact of textual corruption in many passages, and the probability of corruption in many others. The truth is, that besides the two classes of textual difficulties, called *historical* and *grammatical*, there is a third more formidable than either, viz., the class of *literal* difficulties, which may very well be the result of misprinting. Conjectural criticism being thus allowed, it becomes expedient to assign the limits within which it should be exercised. Something towards this end would be accomplished if a code of canons could be imposed upon all, as a common basis of operations. Evidently, such a preliminary would obviate a vast and useless expenditure of inventive sagacity, and the antiquarians would thereby be spared a world of superfluous speculation. There are, indeed, certain considerations which might assist the critics in the determination

of that basis. For one thing, the hopelessness of certain classes of emendations may well be allowed to put them out of court, however felicitous they may be :

1. Where there is no close resemblance between the *ductus literarum* of the word or words to be supplanted, and that of the word or words to be supplied, regard being had either to their written or to their printed form. For example : we cannot expect that, in *As You Like It, tributary streams* will ever be accepted in lieu of 'wearie very means'; that in *All's Well that Ends Well, her own suit joining with her mother's grace,* will ever supersede 'Her insuite comming with her modern grace'; or that, in *The Comedy of Errors, prospice funem* will ever take the place of 'the prophecy.'

2. Where the proposed word is unknown or very unusual in the relative literature : for instance, in 1 *Hen. IV., tame chetah* for 'tame cheater'; in *The Tempest, young chamals* (i. e. Angora goats) for 'young scamels': to which might be added several of the proposed emendations of *strachy,* in *Twelfth Night.* At the same time it should be remembered that some words can more readily substantiate their title than others : e. g., *rother* for 'brother' in *Timon of Athens* is a good word enough, and that it was not wholly unknown to Shakespeare is proved by Rother Street in the very town where he was born and died, the name by which the street was known in his lifetime. Yet no example of the use of *rother,* an ox, has ever been discovered in the literature of his day.

Criticism, like Commentary, has often fallen to the

lot of men whose abilities and training had not fitted them for that kind of intellectual work. In the fifth of De Quincey's *Letters to a young man whose education has been neglected*, Dr Nitsch, the Commentator on Kant, affords a mark for the Opium-Eater's fine irony. He fancies the learned doctor protesting against the reasonableness of expecting a man, who has all this commenting to do, to have thoroughly mastered his author. The equitable division of labour demands that one man shall master the system, and another write commentaries! Criticism offers almost as prominent a mark for ridicule. If a few really intelligent and learned men have done much good work in this department, assuredly the greater bulk of criticism has proceeded from those who had few or none of the necessary requirements. The least one might expect of them would be a study of the context, and the reservation of their speculations until some one conjecture can be shown to *slain* its rivals. Nobody cares to be told that possibly a suspicious word in the text is a misprint for this, that, or the other; as is the custom with several critics of this day, to whom the great Becket seems to have bequeathed the rags which served him for a mantle.

The simple truth is, that successful emendation is the fruit of severe study and research on the one hand, and of rare sensibility and sense on the other. The number of really satisfactory conjectures are comparatively few; and few are those critics who have shown any remarkable sagacity in this kind of speculation.

The ensuing may be cited with unqualified satisfaction:

1. Our Poesie is as a Gowne, which uses
    From whence 'tis nourisht.—*Timon of Athens*, i. 1.
    Our Poesie is as a Gumme (Pope) which oozes (Johnson), &c.

2. It is the Pastour Lards, the Brother's sides,
    The want that makes him leane.—*Ibid.* iv. 3.
    It is the Pasture (Rowe) lards the rother's (Singer) sides,
    The want that makes him leane (Rowe).

3. for thou seest it will not coole my nature.—*Twelfth Night*, i. 3.
    for thou seest it will not curle by (Theobald) nature.

4. Her infinite comming with her moderne grace,
    Subdu'd me to her rate.—*All's Well that Ends Well*, v. 2.
    Her infinite cunning (Walker), &c.

5. Till that the wearie verie meanes do ebbe.—*As You Like It*, ii. 7.
    Till that the wearer's (Singer), &c.

6. To you, our Swords have leaden points, *Mark Antony*:
    Our Armes in strength of malice.—*Julius Cæsar*, iii. 1.
    Our Armes in strength of amitie (Singer) *

---

* Even the proposer of this palmarian emendation was not aware of the corroboration it might receive from Shakespeare's language in other places. We have in *Antony and Cleopatra* the very phrase in one place, and almost the very phrase in another. In ii. 6 we read 'that which is *the strength of their amity* shall prove the immediate author of their variance': and in iii. 2, Antony says,

> I'll *wrestle* with you *in my strength of love*.

Again in 2 *Hen. IV.* 2, we have this parallel,

> Let's drink together friendly, and *embrace*,
> That all their eyes may bear these tokens home
> Of our restored love and *amity:*

In fact, 'malice' in the folio is merely the result of correcting *amitie*, set up awry, with the *m* and *a* transposed. The entire sense is, 'We will receive and embrace you externally, with our arms in all their strength of amity, and internally, with our hearts of brothers' temper'. No other emendation meets all the requirements of the passage.

7.   Thy palenesse moves me more than eloquence.
                            Merchant of Venice, iii. 2.
      Thy plainnesse (Warburton) moves me, &c.

8.   For I do see the cruell pangs of death
      Right in thine eye.—*King John*, iv. 4.
      Riot (Brae) in thine eye.

9.   'Tis enough
      That (Britaine) I have kill'd thy Mistris : Peace,
      He give no wound to thee.—*Cymbeline*, v. 1.
      . . . . . I have kill'd thy Mistris-piece (Staunton)*.

10.   for his Nose was as sharpe as a Pen, and a Table of greene
      fields.— *Hen. V.*, ii. 3.
            . . . . . . and a Babled (Theobald) of greene fields.

11.   For his Bounty,
      There was no winter in 't. An *Anthony* it was,
      That grew the more by reaping.—*Antony and Cleopatra*, v. 2.
                            an autumn 'twas (Theobald).

12.   I have retyr'd me to a wastefull cocke.—*Timon of Athens*, ii. 2.
      I have retyr'd me to a wakefull couche (Swynfen Jervis).

As to the last, a few remarks may be added in justification of so valuable a correction. We do not touch
the fitness or the beauty of the emendation, which speak
for themselves, but the probability of the misprint. We
must use a favourite resource of Zachary Jackson here.
In the 'upper case' of the compositor, the ſt and k are
in contiguous 'boxes', so that an ſt would sometimes be
dropped into the k box by mistake: thus ſt k ; whence
it might very well happen that *wakefull* was set up
waſtefull. Not improbably *wakefull* in the 'copy' sug-

* This master-piece in emendation was communicated to us by Mr
Staunton in the course of conversation, shortly after the completion
of his Edition of *Shakespeare*.

gested *cock* to the mind of the workman instead of *couch*, by the power of association; the barn-cock being often called the wakeful bird, or the wakeful cock. As an illustration of this particular misprint, we may instance these two cases: in one Birmingham newspaper we observed the remarkable expression (of a remarkable phenomenon) 'sermon without bosh', for *sermon without book;* and in another, 'genial break' for *genial breath;* and the blunder of 'break' for *breath* also occurred in one of the proofs of our tractate entitled, *Was Thomas Lodge an Actor?* p. 10.

Of course, in order to appreciate the actual duty done by each of these twelve emendations, it is necessary to make the passage to which it applies a special study. All that the mere presentation of them to the eye can do, is to show the reader that the *ductus literarum* of the conjecture is sufficiently near to that of the text, which is also the fact in the majority of unsuccessful conjectures.

As in the case of 'wastefull' for *wakefull*, in many misprints the process is patent: in some, however, we see the fatality under which certain classes of words were wrongly set up, without being able to see why that fatality existed. Of all classes pronouns (simply as such) were the most commonly misprinted. The first folio of Shakespeare and the first quarto of the *Sonnets* teem with such errors. Some particular passages seem to have suffered from as great a fatality. Again and again has corruption disastered them, misprint being graffed on misprint. Here are two examples:

1. In the *Tempest*, i. 2, it is beyond the shadow of a doubt that Shakespeare wrote,

> Urchins
> Shall forth at vast of night, that they may worke
> All exercise on thee.

Three morsels of knowledge, indeed, are requisite for the full comprehension of the sense: *to forth* was a common phrase for *to go forth*; *vast of night* meant *dead of night*; and *exercise* meant *chastisement*. Ignorance of one or some of these things has hitherto hindered the reception of Mr Thomas White's restoration. It has been argued by a very competent critic and editor, that *exercise* must be a verb, because *to work exercise* would, otherwise, be a pleonasm which it would be impertinent to impute to Shakespeare. Nothing can be more fallacious than that style of argument. Pleonasms are the very stuff of the Elizabethan and Jacobian writers. In our authorized version of the Holy Scriptures, for instance, St Paul is made to say (2 Cor. viii. 11), 'Now therefore, perform ye the doing of it.' But nevertheless, *to work exercise* is not a pleonasm: it means *to inflict punishment*. Unhappily in setting up the text of the *Tempest* in 1622, the 'th' of 'forth' got slightly dislocated, so as to be too near the following word 'at'. Accordingly, the lines stand there

> Urchins
> Shall for that vast of night, that they may worke
> All exercise on thee.

Then came the editors who, seeing in the line in

question an intimation of the awfully indefinite duration
of the night during which the urchins are permitted to
exercise their infernal arts on Caliban—as if, forsooth,
their privilege were limited to a single night, and to one
which was longer than any other—, advanced the
limitary comma from 'night' to 'worke'. Then came
Thomas Warton, who, requiring the line for the illustration of one in Milton, gave it in a note thus:

Urchins
Shall for that want of night that they may work;

thereby graffing one misprint on another.*

2. In his *réchauffé* of the old *Timon*, Shakespeare
undoubtedly wrote,

Our poesie is as a gumme which oozes
From whence 'tis nourisht.

But in the edition of 1623, the passage was, as we have
seen, thus misprinted,

Our Poesie is as a Gowne which uses
From whence 'tis nourisht.

and Tieck, who set himself up as a critic on Shakespeare
and other English Dramatists, defended the nonsense,
under the impression, perhaps, that Shakespeare meant
to compare poetry to a worn-out robe!

Unhappy passage! In a letter on 'The influences
of Newspapers on Education', written by Mr Blanchard
Jerrold, in the *Daily News*, he had intended to quote

* In the former edition of *The Still Lion* the line appears with a
new misprint,

Shall forth at vast of night, that they make worke. See *ante*, p. 39.

the amended version; but to his horror it appeared in a totally new form,

<blockquote>Our poesy is as a queen that dozeth;</blockquote>

and it now remains for some conceited foreigner of the future to contend that the bard meant to signalize the drowsiness of our poetry, by comparing it to a queen, who, despite the calls of her high station, falls asleep on her throne!

Let us now consider three selected passages, given in both the quarto and folio editions of *Hamlet*. These will serve as samples of the state of the old text, and of the value of having more than one version of a passage which has suffered from the blunder of copyist or printer. In the first, the folio corrects the error of the quarto: in the second, the quarto corrects the error of the folio: in the third, the folio deserts us; no quarto-reading can, in this case, be allowed as the correction of another; and conjecture has not arrived at any satisfactory result.

1. In *Hamlet*, iv. 7, as given in the quartos of 1604 and 1605, we have,

<blockquote>
so that my arrowes
Too slightly tymberd for so loued Arm'd,
Would have reuerted to my bowe againe,
But not where I haue [had] aym'd them.
</blockquote>

The only variation in the words 'loued Arm'd' given by the early quartos is, that two read 'loued armes', and one reads 'loved armes'.

Such a crux as that would have been 'larks' or

'nuts' to the critical taste. Happily the folio 1623 gives us the true lection, viz. *loud a Winde*. So Ascham, in his *Toxophilus*, Book ii. (Arber's Reprint, p. 150-1), says, 'The greatest enemy of Shootyng is the winde and wether, &c. Weak bowes, and lyght shaftes can not stande in a rough wynde.'

2. If, on the other hand, we had but the first folio, we should be called upon to *explain* or *amend* the following passage in *Hamlet* :

> To his good Friends, thus wide He ope my Armes :
> And like the kinde Life-rend'ring Politician,
> Repast them with my blood.

Such a crux as 'Life-rend'ring Politician' would have been as appetising and entertaining as the last ; and the game would naturally have been quickened by the fact, that when *Hamlet* was first indited *Politician*, occuring once, however, in this play ('the Pate of a Politician,' iv. 1,) was an *insolens verbum*, which we now believe to have been first used by George Puttenham in 1589, if he were the author (which he probably was) of *The Arte of English Poesie*. The misprint is an unusual expansion of the original word. It is most unlikely that *Pelican* (the word of the quarto editions) was (as some have asserted) a difficulty with the old compositor : on the contrary, we may be pretty sure that he set up *Polician*, and that a pedantic 'reader' of the house improved upon this, converting it into *Politician*.

3. Now for a case in which the old copies concur

to leave us at the mercy of conjecture. In the same quarto editions of *Hamlet* we read,

> For use almost can change the stamp of nature,
> And either the deuill, or throwe him out
> With wonderous potency.

Unhappily this passage, defective by *one* word (probably a verb following on 'either' and governing 'the devill'), is not in the first quarto, nor yet in any of the early folio editions. The defect is so miserably supplied by the dateless quarto (1607) that the modern editor is driven to the conclusion that the word there given is a mere conjecture, and that the defect must be anew conjecturally supplied. This quarto reads :—

> For use almost can change the stamp of nature,
> And maister the deuill, or throwe him out
> With wonderous potency.

Here 'maister' is not only bad on the score of rhythm, but still leaves the line short   Not improbably it was intended to supply the word for which 'either' was conceived to be a misprint. Pope and Capell followed this lead, and read 'And master *even* the devil—' But all other editors have wisely retained 'either': viz. 'And either *curb* the devil' — Malone ; 'And either *quell* the devil'—Singer : while the late Mr Bolton Corney proposed to read, 'And either *aid* the devil'—and Mr Cartwright, 'And either *lay* the devil.' A correspondent of *Notes and Queries* (3rd S. x. 426) signing himself F proposed, 'And either *house* the devil'; conceiving (like Mr Corney) that the missing word should be antithetical to *throw out*, and not perceiving that no very 'wondrous potency' would be required to house a demon, who was already by nature in possession! Two conjectures privately communicated to us deserve mention. Our valued friend, Professor Sylvester, would read 'And either *mask* the devil'—conceiving that 'maister' was a misprint for the true word. In this course he is somewhat countenanced by a passage occurring in a prior speech of Polonius (III. 1):

> We are oft to blame in this,—
> 'Tis too much proved, that with devotion's visage,
> And pious action, we do sugar o'er
> The devil himself.

Another valued friend, Mr C. J. Monro, proposes to read 'And *entertain* the devil'—conceiving that 'either' may be a press error for *entertain*. All other conjectures which I have seen are so utterly imbecile, that I will spare their proposers the ordeal of criticism. It is not easy to discover why the five verbs, *curb, quell, lay, aid,* and *house* found more favour than a score of others, apparently as well suited to the sense and measure of the line as any of those. How soon are the resources of the conjectural critics exhausted! how meagre is the evidence adduced in favour of any single conjecture! yet the requirements of the passage are by no means severe, nor are the means for complying with them either narrow or *recherché*. It is rather an *embarras des richesses* that hinders our decision. To call over a few of the candidates for admission into the text : *curb* suggests *rein, rule, thrall, bind, chain,* &c.; *quell* and *lay* suggest *charm, worst, quench, foil, balk, cross, thwart, daunt, shame, cow,* &c.; while *aid* and *house* suggest *fire, rouse, stir, serve, lodge, feed,* &c. Besides which there are many dissyllables that would answer the purposes of sense and measure, as *abate, abase,* &c. And why not read 'And over-master the devil'—seeing that the word *o'ermaster* occurs in a former scene of this play? We are not now attempting the settlement of this question, but merely pointing out what a wealth of suggestion has been ignored by the self-complacent critics who have so feebly attempted it. But, as a preliminary to its settlement, we venture to call attention to the evident requirements of the passage. 'The stamp of nature' is not new to us in this connection, nor in this play; we have had it twice in the second ghost-scene, viz. the 'vicious mole of nature', and 'the stamp of one defect'. Now Hamlet would say, 'Use almost can change [convert] this stamp of nature': so that an antithesis is not only *not* required, but is impertinent. Use, he would say, can either *subdue* 'habit's devil', by following out his own prescription of *gradual weaning from evil,* or (if the worst come to the worst and revolution be necessary) *cast him out:* and either of these can such use, or change of habit, effect 'with wondrous potency.' The key-note of the whole passage is 'Reformation, by gradually subduing evil habits'; and so far from Hamlet's advice, 'assume a virtue if you have it not', being (as Knight understood

it) a recommendation of hypocrisy, 'the homage paid by
vice to virtue', it is given solely with the view of facili-
tating inward amendment, and is therefore honest and
sincere.   Very similar advice was given by Lewis Vives
in a book which, not improbably, may have been Shakespeare's closet-companion, viz. *The Introduction to
Wysedom:* Englished by Richarde Morysine: 1540, Sig.
B. ii.

> 'Let every man desyre uprighte thinges, and flee the
> crooked: chose the good, and refuse the evyll, *this
> use and custome shall tourne well doinge almost into
> nature,* and so worke, that none, but suche as are
> compelled, and suche as are in stryfe, found the
> weaker, shall be brought to do evyll.'

Roger Ascham, too, in his *Toxophilus,* 1545, Book ii.
(Arber's Reprint, p. 141), has the same proposition in
somewhat different words   . .

> 'And in stede of the fervent desyre, which provoketh
> a chylde to be better than hys felowe, lette a man
> be as muche stirred up with shamefastnes to be
> worse than all other. * * * * * And hereby you
> may se that that is true whiche Cicero sayeth, *that
> a man by use, may be broughte to a newe nature.*'

This, in fact, is exactly what is meant in Sir Joshua
Reynolds' *Fifteenth Discourse,* where we are recom-
mended 'to feign a relish till we find a relish come, and
feel that what began in fiction terminates in reality'.

The missing word, then, must at least import *the*

subduing of the devil of habit. In the first quarto we
have the expression,

> 'And win [i. e. wean] yourself by little as you may',

from the sin to which you [the queen] have habituated
yourself. Now, that *weaning by little and little*, or
gradually weaning the will and affections from the cus-
tomary sin, 'recurring and suggesting still', is just what
the missing word, were it recovered, would assuredly be
found to express or to imply. *Lay* and *shame* are
equally acceptable in sense, and both afford a perfect
rhythm. Perhaps *shame* is the finer reading of the two.
At the same time, it must be owned, that Hamlet's prescription is calculated to do but little for the sinner:
at best, we fear, to 'skin and film the rancorous place.'
Kant well says:

> 'People usually set about this matter [i.e. the reform-
> ation of character] otherwise, fighting against par-
> ticular vices, and leaving the common root whence
> they sprout untouched. And yet mankind * * *
> is just so much the more readily awakened to
> a profounder reverence for duty, the more he
> is taught to exclude therefrom all foreign motives
> that self-love might (otherwise) foist into the
> maxims of conduct.'

We can hardly say that conjecture has yet determined the best reading here; though it cannot be said
that sufficient indications are wanting for its guidance.
Unfortunately it is in the very nature of the case, that

some doubt should continue to vex this passage, after conjecture has done its work.

Let us take a more striking case than this: a passage in which there is no *hiatus:* merely a misprint; which has nevertheless all the features of incurable corruption. We refer to that famous Rope-scarre which occurs at the opening of the fifth act of *Much Ado about Nothing.* Leonato, refusing the proffered consolations of his brother, says,

> Bring me a father that so lov'd his childe,
> Whose joy of her is overwhelm'd like mine,
> And bid him speake of patience

Ritson reads the last line,

> And bid him speake *to me* of patience,

and the late Mr Barron Field independently suggested the same, unnecessary, if not impertinent, interpolation. Leonato continues, after four lines which we omit here,

> If such a one will smile and stroke his beard,
> And sorrow, wagge, crie hem, when he should grone,
> Patch grief with proverbs, make misfortune drunke,
> With candle-wasters · bring him yet to me,
> And I of him will gather patience:
> But there is no such man, &c.—Folio 1623.

The line, 'And I *of him* will gather patience', doubt-less suggested the conjecture of Ritson and Barron Field. The argument is this: 'Find me a man who has suffered my calamity; and if he will speak of patience, I, on my part, will gather patience of him'. In the passage lastly quoted there are two difficulties. The first was plausibly bridged over by Steevens by simply transposing 'And' and 'erie,' 'wagge' meaning, according to this interpretation, as it does in so many other places, *budge*. The objection to this is, that it is inconsistent with the philosophic and serious character of the person whom Leonato invests with his own wrongs and sorrows. The second difficulty concerns the obsolete word 'candle-wasters'. Here, then, is a passage which demands both emendation and exposition : but in order to deal with it successfully, we must first cope with the second difficulty. Of all the commentators, Zachary Jackson alone proposed an emendation for 'candle-wasters': he conjectured *candle-waters!* What it means it is hard to say ; for no such word is known to have ever existed, though *candle*, a sort of posset, is familiar enough. We remember that Eden Warwick (i. e. the late Mr George Jabet, the accomplished editor of *The Poet's Pleasaunce*, 1847) proposed to substitute for Hamlet's *pajock* or *paiocke* the strange word *patokie*, a word he had coined expressly for the occasion, as a possible derivative of *patacco* or *patoikoi*. We need not pause to consider the merit or demerit of such singular suggestions, both being non-suited for something even worse than *insolentia*. But, regarding 'candle-wasters' as a genuine word, what was its meaning? Mr Staunton (Ed. vol. i. p. 730) says that it means 'Bacchanals, revellers'. Mr Dyce follows suit. I venture to think that these editors have gone beyond the voucher of their authorities. We do not believe that a single example can be adduced of *candle-waster* in that sense.

It is to us passing strange that the word 'drunk' in this passage should have been uniformily interpreted in its literal sense, and 'candle-wasters' understood to mean drunkards, who spend the night in revelling. Of all absurd things, there is nothing more painfully absurd than the attempt to literalize a metaphor. Surely Shakespeare never meant Leonato to deny the possibility of his drowning his troubles in drink; for that were the easiest as it is the most vulgar resource of a man in trouble. Nanty Ewart, in *Redgauntlet*, is such a man. Drunkenness was his resource from the misery of haunting memories. 'Here is no lack of my best friend', said Ewart, on taking out his flask, after awakening an old sorrow, the remembrance of which was too painful to be borne with patience. Whatever, then, was meant by 'making misfortune drunk with candle-wasters', it must have been some achievement which in Leonato's circumstances was very difficult of performance; so difficult that he pronounced it impossible. Now, Whalley succeeded in unearthing two examples of the use of *candle-waster* and *lamp-waster*, and one of *candle-wasting*, which throw considerable light on this passage; but which, from their rebutting the ordinary interpretation, are usually suppressed by the editors. Here they are .

Heart, was there ever so prosperous an invention thus unluckily prevented and spoiled by a whoreson book-worm or *candle-waster?*
Ben Jonson : *Cynthia's Revells*, iii. 2.

He should more catch your delicate court-ear, than all your head-scratchers, thumb-biters, *lamp-wasters* of them all.
Shakerley Marmion : *The Antiquary*, 1641, 4to.

I which have known you better and more inwardly than a thousand of these *candle-wasting* book-worms.

> The Hospitall of Incurable Fooles: Erected in English, as near the first Italian modell and platforme, as the unskilfull hand of an ignorant Architect could devise. 1600, sm. 4to. Sig. H.

From these extracts we gather that a *candle-waster* is a *book-worm* ; literally, a consumer of the ' midnight oil ', a nocturnal student ; and the term (like ' Grub-street ' of a century later) was always applied contemptuously, and the work of such a writer was said, after the Latin phrase, *to smell of the lamp.** Not improbably the term meant also a *lucubration.* The conclusion is, that *to make misfortune drunk with candle-wasters*, is *to drown one's troubles in study ;* and what fitter pendant could be found to the preceding phrase to ' patch grief with pro-verbs ' ?

So far, then, all is clear and indisputable. We may now recur to the former part of Leonato's speech, in which the real crux lies :

> If such a one will smile and stroke his beard,
> And sorrow, wagge, crie hem, when he should grone, &c.

To stroke the beard and cry hem ! (what the French call *faire le sérieux*) is the very picture of a sententious pedant who would talk down or scold down the first gush of natural feeling, whether of grief or of rage.

---

* *Lucernam olet.* Again, *Oleum perdere* is to lose one's labour in writing, to be an oil-waster. Dryden, in his Preface to *Troilus and Cressida*, 1679, 8vo, falls foul of Shakespeare for *catachresis ;* and in the same breath speaks of certain dramas smelling of the buskin ! As buskins are not remarkable for their offensive odour, the phrase is a worse *catachresis* than is to be found in Shakespeare.

Such was Achilles' epitome of Nestor in *Troilus and Cressida*, i. 3, where that chief is described as amusing himself with Patroclus' mimicry of the Greeks :

> Now play me Nestor ; hem and stroke thy beard !

It seems to follow, then, that the words 'And sorrow wagge' must be an error for some phrase expressive of choking, smothering, or suppressing sorrow   Hence we venture to think, that, supposing there has been no dislocation of the text, Tyrwhitt's conjecture of *gagge* for 'wagge' at least preserves the continuity of the thought, and the integrity of the image, as well as the *ductus literarum*.   To attempt to settle the question definitely in favour of this or that conjecture would at present be mere waste of time.   The interpretation we have given to the purport of the passage cannot, we are assured, be successfully assailed ; and that may help the critic to a solution of the textual difficulty.

Mr Staunton, who found, as we have said, a bacchanalian allusion in the phrase *to make misfortune drunk with candle-wasters*, persuaded himself that the former part of the speech bears out that view.   He contended that to 'cry hem' here means, to sing the burden of a roystering song *   To all which we say, (1.) that no example of either the one or the other phrase, employed in those senses, has ever been adduced ; (2.) that if a dozen examples in point were found, the case would be in no wise mended ; for the interpretation in question is logic-

---

* Possibly 'Hem boys!' in *II. Hen. IV.*, iii. 2, is part of such a refrain.

ally inconsistent with the context. The counsel Leonato is rejecting, is that he should seek to restrain and assuage his grief, rather than indulge it. To reply, as we contend he is intended to do, 'Show me a man who has my weight of sorrow and wrong, and is yet an example of stoical or cheerful endurance, and I will follow your counsel,' is logical and *ad rem :* but to reply, 'Show me a man who, having as great a sorrow or wrong as I have, drowns the remembrance of it in drunken revelry,' &c., would be wholly irrelevant : and this for four reasons, which are here set forth at length :—

i. Because it would imply that Antonio had been recommending drunkenness to his brother, as an infallible specific for grief : for it would make Leonato's words imply that if a man could be produced who had succeeded in that feat, he would accede to his brother's suggestion, and make such a man his model : only 'patience' would be an outstanding difficulty.

ii. Because it would make Leonato say, 'Show me a man who has so little patience and self-control as to rush to the tap-room for the solace of his troubles, and I will make him my model, and gather patience of him,' which would be an impossible task.

iii. Because it would make him assert that there is no such man : that no man could be found who, having Leonato's sorrow or wrong, could succeed in forgetting it in drinking-bouts : whereas drink is, as we have seen, the common resource of common men in trouble.

iv. Because it would confound the intellectual man

with him who lacks intellect, industry, and moral feeling. As Mrs Beecher-Stowe so well puts it in *Dred* (chap. x.), 'Every one [who is 'uncomfortable and gloomy'] naturally inclines towards *some* source of consolation. *He who is intellectual reads and studies;* he who is industrious flies to business; he who is affectionate seeks friends; he who is pious, religion; *but he who is none of these—what has he but his whiskey?*' It is thus that the common sense of our time throws light upon the dark or doubtful passages in Shakespeare. But this particular *crux* is, in our opinion, one of the least doubtful *in drift*, though it has been so persistently perverted by commentators of the literalizing school.

We may here cite a few other instances of the supreme value of modern illustration, as an aid to emendation and interpretation (we gave two at pp. 99 and 153). We have already noted the plausibility of *bed* as an emendation of 'bone' in that famous speech of Alcibiades, which Mr Dyce printed without an attempt to defend or explain it. Addressing the doting Senators (behind their backs), the General exclaims,

> Now the Gods keepe you old enough,
> That you may live
> Onely in bone, that none may looke on you.
> *Timon*, iii. 5, Folio 1623.

That the *one* in 'bone' was caught by the compositor from the *one* in 'onely', is probable, regard being had to the proximity of 'none'. Surely, their fitting place was *bed*, where the ailments of their advanced age might receive all needful ministrations, and where they would be safe from bringing disgrace on the government of Athens. In this reading we are supported by a passage in Mr George Dawson's address to his Congregation, on the occasion of celebrating the twenty-fifth anniversary of 'The Church of the Saviour' at Birmingham, delivered there on Aug. 5, 1872. He said, in reference to his own late illness,

> 'To be patient with a man who has always something the matter with him is one of the grandest kinds of patience. People always ailing are tiresome, there is no denying it. I have a great dread of becoming an invalid. I have a great respect for invalids *in bed,—out of sight.*'

i. e. 'Only in bed, that none may look on [them]'. Can a more light-giving illustration be conceived?

Then, apart from emendation, how 'express and admirable' is the following from a modern novelist, now deceased, as determining the sense of an obscure phrase in *Hamlet*, i. 1. Bernardo asks, 'What, is Horatio there?' To which Horatio replies, 'A piece of him.' The late Charles Knight speaks of this as Horatio's 'familiar pleasantry' but what is its meaning? The simple answer is—Horatio calls his hand, as he touches that of the Prince—a piece of himself, because he could not be distinctly seen in the dark shade of the battlement: i. e. a piece, as implying that the rest was there, though not revealed to Hamlet's sense at once. Now all this is suggested by a passage in the penultimate chapter of *Jane Eyre.* She has come upon the blind Rochester, and placed her hand in his :

> "'Her very fingers', he cried, 'her small, slight
> fingers ! *If so, there must be more of her*'."

Of course, neither Charlotte **Brontë** nor Mr George Dawson had the faintest notion of illustrating Shakespeare, when these things were uttered. If either of them had, some of the force of the illustration would be lost. As it is, we see the power of common sense, even in this day, to do the great playwright yeoman's service. Just so does a fine passage in Mr Caird's sermon, entitled *Religion in Common Life*, p. 24, afford a guiding light for all who care to determine the exact thought which was in Shakespeare's mind when he wrote that passage, in the *Tempest*, iii. 1, which is so corruptly given in the folio 1623 :

> **I forget ;**
> But these sweet thoughts, doe even refresh my labours,
> Most busie lest, when I doe it.

Mr Caird says,

'The thought of all this may dwell, a latent joy, a hidden motive, deep down in his heart of hearts, may come rushing in, a sweet solace, at every pause of exertion, and act like a secret oil to smooth the wheels of labour.' Certainly Shakespeare meant to say that *the sweet thoughts well up in the pauses of exertion*. Had not Dr Wellesley overlooked this, he would not have applied 'most' to 'refresh', and 'busy' to Ferdinand (*Stray Notes*, 1865, p. 2), making him say that his sweet thoughts refresh him by their presence during his labours. We would adopt Mr Bullock's reading, *busiliest* for 'busie lest', and regulate the passage thus:

> I forget [i. e. I am forgetting my injunction],
> But these sweet thoughts doe even refresh my labours
> Most busiliest when I doe it. [i. e. do forget it.]

Busiliest may have been written *busielest* (we note that *easiliest* is printed *easilest* in *Cymbeline*, iv. 2): and if so the only error in the folio is a slight dislocation in that word. But here, as in the *crux* from *Much Ado about Nothing*, the question does not admit of a final decision. In such, and the like, we must be content to suspend our judgment, and exercise patience.

In a multitude of cases, however, the correction of the text is certain; and in some, where the remedy is still somewhat doubtful, a particular emendation which has met with all but universal acceptance by the editors has been now and then pronounced too good for the place! It is an exceptional honour for the conjectural critic to be esteemed almost equal to his author. Such was the approbation bestowed by Dr Johnson on Warburton for his emendation of *God*, *vice* 'good', in *Hamlet*, ii 2: 'being a good kissing carrion'; but surely approbation was never so extravagant as in this opinion; for, as Mr Corson points out, 'a good kissing carrion' is simply a carrion that is good for kissing! The highest honour, however, attainable by the author of an emendation was actually attained by Theobald, viz. that of being confounded with his author, and that by no ordinary critic. In our opinion he fully deserved that honour, and stands *facile princeps* among the host of conjectural critics. Holding that opinion, we indignantly repel Dr Johnson's censure on Theobald; whom he calls 'a man of narrow comprehension and small acquisitions, with no native and intrinsic splendour of genius, with little of the artificial light of learning, but zealous for minute accuracy, and not negligent in pursuing it.' But, as if grudging Theobald this small concession, he adds that Theobald was 'weak and ignorant', 'mean and faithless', 'petulant and ostentatious'. De Quincey, echoing Johnson, calls Theobald 'painstaking but dull': (*Works*, Black, vol. vi. p. 126, note); and yet, on another occasion, when De Quincey is insisting on 'the gratitude of our veneration for Shakespeare', he actually adduces, as a remarkable display of Shakespeare's dramatic art, the famous words 'and a babled of green fields', from Mrs Quickly's description of Falstaff's death, in *Hen. V.*, ii. 3. Those words, he thinks, 'must have been read by many a thousand with tears and smiles at the same instant'; 'I mean,' he adds, 'connecting them with a previous knowledge of Falstaff and of Mrs Quickly' (*Works*, Black, vol. xiii. p. 119). Just so: that is precisely where lies the marvel of this piece of work, which we owe to Theobald rather than to Shakespeare. I am far from denying that those words are what Shakespeare wrote: indeed, it is the peculiar merit

of that emendation that most probably it exactly restores the original work of the bard : but Theobald had to work upon the corrupt text, 'and a Table of greene fields', which seems to promise so little poetry or knowledge of human nature, that one critic is satisfied that they are a stage direction, incorporated, by mistake, with the text of Mrs Quickly's speech ; another supposes the reference to be to a pen lying on a table-book of green fell ; while Mr Collier's pseudo-old Corrector alters the words into 'on a table of green frieze.' *
Hopeless indeed must the prosaic corruption appear to most men—to all who have not caught the infection of Shakespeare's genius, and have not a like knowledge of human nature. Theobald, however, proved himself to have had both. He knew precisely how Falstaff would talk, when he lay picking the bed-clothes, and smiling on his fingers' ends ; and he knew exactly what part of his babbling talk would be remembered and repeated by Mrs Quickly. Moreover, he had faith in Shakespeare, and believed that he would reproduce all this ; and he had moreover the necessary knowledge of Elizabethan orthography, such as this, that *babbled* was ordinarily spelt *babled*. Thus was he led to an emendation which has covered Shakespeare with glory and been identified with his text. (See *Notes and Queries*, 1st S. viii. 314, for an eloquent commentary on this scene,

* He must have been reading Brewster's *Optics*, 1831, p. 296, where the author proposes an observation, on 'a pen lying upon a green cloth.'

written in the vein of Dr John Brown; and also *The Grammar of Assent*, pp. 264—270, where Dr Newman takes the corrupt passage of the folio, with its various emendations, as the concrete example of complex inference.)

No amount of sagacity or ingenuity in the critic can compensate the want of appropriate learning and scholarship. In some instances, indeed, if he have sagacity to catch the hidden sense of a corrupt passage, and ingenuity in conjecture, a great step may be made towards its restoration. But success in any case presupposes the appropriate knowledge Dr E. A. Abbott's elaborate but still imperfect *Shakespearian Grammar* will at least serve to testify to the fact that the grammar of Shakespeare and his contemporaries is not at all that of our written tongue, and Dyce's *Glossary*, and Dr Alexander Schmidt's *Shakespeare-Lexicon* (of which at present but one volume has been published), will afford abundant evidence of the fact that there was a treasury of words open to an Elizabethan writer, which are now obsolete, or at least current in senses more or less different from those which the words imported in the fourteenth and fifteenth centuries.

For other aids to conjecture in the vindication or the restoration of the text, one of the most valuable is the collation of passages more or less parallel, occurring in Shakespeare's plays and poems. For example: in *Timon of Athens*, iii. 3, Sempronius exclaims,

How? Have they deny'de him?
Has Ventidgius and Lucullus deny'de him,

> And does he send to me? Three *? Humh?
> It showes but little love, or judgement in him.
> Must I be his last Refuge? His Friends (like Physitians)
> Thrive, give him over: Must I take th' Cure upon me?

The mention of Lucius, Lucullus, and Ventidius (explaining the ejaculation 'Three'), has been thought to favour Johnson's conjecture, that 'thrive' is a misprint for *thrice*: q. d. these three friends have one after another given him over, just as physicians give over their patient. But a parallel passage in the fourth act of the same play seems to us quite sufficient to justify the text as it stands in the folio. Timon addressing the banditti, says,

> Trust not the physitian,
> His Antidotes are poyson, and he slayes
> More then you Rob: Take wealth, and lives together, &c.

i. e. he advises the robbers to take the physicians as their examples, who thrive by their patients' wealth first, and leave them to die of their drugs afterwards. We maintain, then, that in the former place Sempronius is intended to say, that Timon's friends act by him as physicians do by their patients, *thrive* by him, and then *give him over*. Till the singular force of this parallel can be explained away, it is an impertinence to treat the suspected passage as corrupt.

Another case, where a passage ought to help us to restore an undoubtedly corrupt text, is in *Measure for Measure*. Escalus says,

* i. e. with Lucius.

> Well, heaven forgive him ; and forgive us all
> *Some rise by sinne, and some by vertue fall*
> Some run from brakes of Ice, and answer none,
> And some condemned for a fault alone.

The second line being in italics in the folio 1623, we may safely regard these three lines as the vestiges of an older play, or as an interpolation by an inferior hand : but certainly they must have had sense once ; while at present the line following that in italics is quite innocent of meaning. Apparently 'and answer none' means, *and are not called to account ;* since in the last line we are told that judgment is passed on others for a single fault. Accordingly one would expect to find that the corrupt line means, that *some run through a course of increasing wickedness, without being called to account.* Now there is a passage in *Cymbeline,* v. 1, which is of good service to us at this pinch. Posthumus says, addressing the Gods,

> But alacke,
> You snatch some hence for little faults   that's love
> To have them fall no more : you some permit
> To second illes with illes, each elder worse, &c.

We have here the same counter-assertions, but in the reverse order. Reading them thus,

> You some permit
> To second illes with illes, each elder worse,
> You snatch some hence for little faults ;

and comparing this with the passage from *Measure for Measure,* we can hardly help believing, that the corrupt line

Some run from brakes of Ice, and answer none,

ought to assert, that some run through a long career of sin going on ever from bad to worse, without being called to account. Without some further *datum* it is hardly possible to propose a satisfactory emendation of the passage. 'Ice' may, indeed, be *Vice*, as Rowe suggested; or it may be *Ille* or *Illes*, or even *Sin*, but the *evar* is still obstinately irreducible. At any rate, it is remarkable that the passage in *Cymbeline* should afford an exact analogue to the line which in the folio is printed in italics,

Some rise by sin, and some by virtue fall.

The line following 'each elder worse' is undoubtedly corrupt, viz.

To make them dread it, to the doer's thrift;

but we know well enough what it ought to *mean*, though we have not yet discovered what it ought to *say*: it should mean, that the Gods allow the sinner to run his course, that, in the event, like the prodigal son, his stomach may rise against the husks and wash, and that he may voluntarily return to a cleanly life. Such *rise by sin*; while those who *fall by virtue* are snatched away that they may fall no more. It is, we think, quite probable that by the aid of this analogy the corrupt line may be some day restored. At present it must remain a case of inchoate restoration, like the *sorrow-way* and *busie-lest* passages, which demands patient consideration, not immediate decision.

Here, however, is one from *Coriolanus*, ii. 1, which contains two corruptions, the latter admitting of an easy and conclusive remedy. Let us premise that 'him' here means Martius, not the Baby.

> Your prattling Nurse
> Into a rapture lets her Baby crie,
> While she chats him.

'Chats him' is undoubtedly corrupt; and many conjectures have been made, all alike inadmissible. Perhaps '*claps* him' is the best, but the metre halts for it. As to the other place, Mr Justice Blackstone (*Shakespeare Society's Papers*, i. 99) remarks, 'A RAPTURE is an odd effect of crying in Babies. Dr * * * would read it RUPTURE. Only Qu. If crying ever produces *this* Effect?' To which he adds, 'I have since enquired, and am told that it is usual.' Probably most fathers and mothers know that such is the fact. But Blackstone might have learned it from a sixteenth century work, viz. *Phioravante's Secrets*, 1582, p. 5, where we read,

> 'To helpe yong Children of the Rupture.

The Rupture is caused two waies, the one through weaknesse of the place, and the other through much criyng.'

This emendation was independently proposed by two other critics (see the Cambridge Edition of *Shakespeare*, vi. 316); and it seems as good as an emendation can be; yet it has never been adopted, because it was conceived that the word in the text admitted of explanation and defense. Certainly 'rapture' is just *seizure*: cf. Chapman's *Iliad*, xxii. (Taylor's ed. ii.; 192); and *Pericles*, ii. 1, where 'rupture' is, as was pointed out by Dr Sewell, an error of the press for *rapture*:

> And spite of all the rupture of the sea,
> This jewel holds his biding on my arm.

Mr J. P. Collier (*Farther Particulars*, 1839, p. 41) quotes the parallel passage from the novel on which Shakespeare's play was founded: the hero says he got to land 'with a jewell, whom all the *raptures* of the sea could not bereave from his arme.' But there seems no authority for the employment of *rapture* in the sense of *fit* or *convulsion*: and that being so, we adhere to Blackstone's emendation, and believe that just as *rapture* in *Pericles* was misprinted *rupture*, so *rupture* in *Coriolanus* was misprinted *rapture*.

We conclude this essay with a restoration which is not due to conjectural ingenuity, but to the contemporary authority of Ben Jonson. According to him, Shakespeare, in his *Julius Cæsar*, iii. 1, wrote as follows:

Cæsar.   Thy brother by decree is banished:
          If thou dost bend and pray and fawn for him,
          I spurn thee like a cur out of my way.
Metellus.   Cæsar, thou dost me wrong.
Cæsar.   Cæsar did never wrong but with just cause,
          Nor without cause will he be satisfied.
Metellus.   Is there no voice more worthy than my own, &c.;

and somewhat later (iii. 2) we read,

Second Citizen.   If thou consider rightly of the matter.

> Cæsar has had great wrong.
>
> *Third Citizen.*   Has he, master?

But the folio, our only authority for *Julius Cæsar*, does not give Metellus' remark, but continues Cæsar's address thus,

> Know, Cæsar doth not wrong, nor without cause
> Will he be satisfied

Now this is *à propos* of nothing.   There is nothing in Cæsar's speech preceding these two lines to lead to the denial, 'Cæsar doth not wrong' (for Metellus does not provoke it); and besides, the second line is unfinished.

To Ben Jonson's *Timber or Discoveries; made upon men and matter: &c.* (Works, 1640-1, fol., vol. ii. pp. 97), we are indebted for the preservation of the original text in iii. 1, as we have given it.   But the editors, deeming its adoption an act of unfaithfulness to the folio, will not have it.   Mr Halliwell indeed says (*Life of Shakespeare*, 1848, p. 185), 'Take Jonson's words as literally true, and the whole becomes clear', &c.; and he has a like note on the text, in his magnificent Folio Edition of Shakespeare: but he had not the courage to act on his conviction, and regulate the text on Jonson's authority.   Pope had the temerity to propose substituting for the reply of the Third Citizen, in iii. 2, the altered line,

> Cæsar had never wrong, but with just cause.

Thus making the plebeian a sympathiser with Brutus. The text in iii. 1, as we have first given it, was charged upon Shakespeare as a bull; but Ben Jonson does not tell us that Shakespeare changed it in consequence; nor have we any reason for believing that he would have cared for the laughter of his censors. *Nostro judicio* Ben's critique is captious. The justice of the cause is not inconsistent with wrong. Mr Halliwell rightly observes, 'If *wrong* is taken in the sense of *injury* * or *harm*, as Shakespeare sometimes uses it, there is no absurdity in the line, "He shall have wrong," II. *Hen. VI.*, v. 1.' (*Life of Shakespeare*, 1848, p. 185) Again, in *A Winter's Tale*, v. 1, Paulina, speaking of the hapless Queen, says,

> Had one such power,
> She had just cause.
> *Leontes.*   She had, and would incense me
> To murther her I married.

(i. e. her whom he might take as his second wife). Clearly, then, the Queen has, in Leontes' judgment, *just cause* to incite him to do another a grievous wrong. This is even more amenable to Jonson's censure than the line which fell under it. The Cambridge editors most absurdly charge Jonson with a lapse of memory; and this, too, in the face of the additional facts, that the folio reading is defective both in sense and in measure, and that Jonson reverts to the same censure in the *Induction* to his *Staple of News.*

Where then was the blunder? We say it was Jonson's, and his fellow censors': that the line they laughed at was and is unimpeachable good sense, and that it is

* *Injury*, here, is an instance of the same ambiguity.

the editor's duty to use Jonson's censure for the purpose of correcting the folio reading, and restoring the passage to that form in which, as we believe, it flowed from the pen of Shakespeare.

With anything but pleasing auguries we bring this somewhat desultory essay to a close. Though wishing to treat our opponents with all the ceremony prescribed by the law of arms, we have not been loath to strike in earnest, in support and vindication of a literary heritage which is, in our eyes, far too precious to be made the sport of every ingenious guesser, whose vanity impels him to turn critic or editor. There are early dramatic works enough for such men to try their 'prentice-hands upon, without intruding into that paradise ' where angels fear to tread.' For the fashion of this day in dealing with the text of Shakespeare we have no kind of respect, scarcely any tolerance. We have yet to learn what right a combination of dulness, ignorance, arrogance, and bad taste has to respectful usage ; and of such stuff are the later critics of Shakespeare made, with a few honourable exceptions. Of the mass of their rubbish we have taken no kind of note in the foregoing discussions. In a few select cases we have endeavoured, with such knowledge and ability as we possess, to show how superior is the old text to the readings by which it has been proposed to supersede it ; and where we may have failed in the performance of our task, we have sufficient faith in that text to charge ourselves with the whole blame of the failure.

PUBLISHED NOTICES.

Extract from the Second Annual Volume of the German Shakespeare Society: Preface, p. viii.

" Karl Elze by his treatise, 'Shakespeare's Significance for the present times,' spiced by polemics, leads over to the domain of philological criticism, which is represented this year by two renowned scholars—the Englishman, C. M. Ingleby, and by our countryman, Nicolaus Delius.

" Ingleby, to whom we are indebted for the most complete view and exposure of the Shakespeare Forgeries, which made so much stir in the world at their time, gives us here, as the precursor of a larger work, contributions for the restoration of the Shakesperian text. I have considered it unnecessary to translate his essay, because the principal contents of it would, even in a German garment, remain unintelligible to any one not acquainted with the English language."

Extract from The Saturday Review of July 20, 1867.

" Under the eccentric title of 'the Still Lion,' Dr Ingleby indites an essay on the conjectural emendation of the Text [of Shakspeare], which abounds in robust, pithy sense, jocose humour, and felicitous illustration. There is also enough personality to remind us that the Shakspearian critics of this country are a quarrelsome brood."

JOHN CHILDS AND SON, PRINTERS.